THE SWEET LITTLE BOOK OF

Cupcakes

By NICHOLAS PERUZZI,
with COURTNEY FORRESTER
of Sweet Cupcakes, Inc.

SWEET CUPCAKES *photographs*
by ERIC LEVIN

PETER PAUPER PRESS
White Plains, New York

DEDICATION

To the entire *Sweet* team, for making each day
Sweeter than the last, especially Rob McLeod and
Emily Bao for their confectionery contributions

Designed by Heather Zschock

Sweet Cupcakes photographs by Eric Levin

Additional photographs © Shutterstock
(specific credits inside back cover)

Copyright © 2010
Peter Pauper Press, Inc.
202 Mamaroneck Avenue
White Plains, NY 10601
All rights reserved
ISBN 978-1-4413-0351-6
Printed in Hong Kong
7 6 5

Visit us at www.peterpauper.com

THE SWEET LITTLE BOOK OF

Cupcakes

CONTENTS

INTRODUCTION

Cupcakes are pretty, precious, and perhaps perfect. However, there's more to cupcakes than meets the eye. Although the single-serve treat may be simple in its conception—one origin of the name comes from its most basic cup by cup recipe—cupcakes are a mosaic of flavors fit for any palate. With the unique recipes and techniques in this little book, you will impress your family and friends with your seemingly simple, yet delicious, creations and countless possibilities. You may even get the chance to set aside some time to delight in the fruits of your labor. Sweet!

Derived from the veritable treasure trove of recipes at *Sweet Cupcakes*, Boston's premiere cupcakery, this little cookbook instructs and inspires your inner boutique baker. *Sweet* offers perfection in confection, and here they share their sweet secrets. Over 25 recipes for frostings and fillings, easy decorating ideas and tips, plus 17 recipes for the cakes themselves create an endless array of cupcake possibilities, such as the vanilla Sweet Cake, the refreshing summer flavor, Strawberry Shortcake, or the decadent holiday favorite, Chocolate Pomegranate. Whether you're celebrating a birthday, creating an elegant display for a bridal shower, baking for Halloween trick-or-treaters, or hosting a dinner party, cupcakes are the sweetest addition and a fun and fabulous way to show your guests that they're special.

You can recreate the boutique cupcakery experience with *Sweet's* scrumptious cupcakes for all seasons and occasions.

Why cupcakes? The dessert pairs simplicity with complexity, comfort with creativity, retro with right now, and there's nothing like having your cake and eating it, too!

RECIPE FOR SUCCESS

To use this book, simply peruse the finished "Sweet Treats" cupcake creations in the first chapter, divided into sections by season, including a section of timeless favorites for year-round indulgence. Once you've chosen a "Sweet Treat" cupcake to make, refer to each component— cupcake, filling, and frosting— in each respective chapter, follow the directions to assemble all these scrumptious components together to achieve the finished "Sweet Treat," and *Voilà!* Cupcake Nirvana!

IT'S ELEMENTARY

It's Elementary

No two kitchens are the same, of course. Whether your stove is currently serving as spare closet space or churning out army portions daily, the elements of cupcake baking—ingredients, tools, and techniques—are foolproof! Your first step? Read the entire recipe all the way through before you begin baking. That way you can ensure that you will have all of the necessary ingredients and tools right at your fingertips when they are called for.

It's What's Inside That Counts

Cupcakes truly are the sum of their parts, and they deserve to be pampered with the best you can afford. As with all dishes and desserts, fresh, quality ingredients yield quality flavors. At any grocery store, you should be able to find the basics—butter, sugar, eggs, flour, and baking powder. If you're not afraid of a little challenge, you may want to make your way around local farmers' markets and specialty shops, where you can find high-end sugars, flours, chocolates, and exciting extracts. A note about extracts vs. "flavors": For vanilla, extract is always best. But for some of the recipes, "flavors" will be listed as ingredients, which are different from extracts. You can purchase flavors at many specialty shops, or try online at *www.naturesflavors.com* or *www.thebakerskitchen.net*. Another resource is Formaggio Kitchen, a Boston-area favorite that ships products nationally. Visit them at *www.formaggio kitchen.com*.

Mix It, Bake It, Cake It

With the recent explosion of cupcake paraphernalia on the market, you should have no trouble finding all the necessary (and even unnecessary) accoutrements. To start, you will need the usual baking supplies—a spatula, whisk, wooden spoon, egg beater, electric mixer, bowls, sifter, and measuring cups and spoons. The item that defines the cupcake is, of course, the cupcake tin, which comes in a variety of sizes. *All of the cupcakes in this book, with the exception of the mini pupcakes, are meant to be baked in a standard cupcake tin—they are the perfect portion and will allow adequate space for filling and embellishing.* And don't forget cupcake liners to bake in! Grocery stores and specialty shops carry a variety of cupcake papers, so you can add a touch of color or pattern at the base or bake in a plain white cup, letting you go wild with color on top!

Please note that we have made every effort to ensure that the yields listed are accurate, but each recipe's yield can vary depending on how the batter is distributed in the cupcake tins.

Heatin' Up the Kitchen

Now that you have everything you need to bake, there's the never-ending oven issue to contend with. From altitude to aptitude, each oven can be a little different. Show your oven who's boss by learning its nuances, and you can avoid a scorcher. Always keep an eye on your cupcakes while baking, as cooking times will vary depending on your oven. Many find a cake tester or the readily-available toothpick to be a great cheat tactic. When it pulls out clean, your cupcakes are baked to perfection!

The Icing on the Cake

For decorating ideas and techniques, see pages 120-51. To frost and decorate your cupcakes, you will need standard pastry bags and tips. You can find these in specialty shops, or a simple set might be found in your local grocery store. There are so many different ways to add pizzazz to a simple cupcake, including drizzles, crumbles, and other toppings. Let your creativity take hold and, most of all, have fun!

Meet the Sweet Treats—
Finished Cupcake Creations

Perennial Favorites
Spring Cupcakes in Bloom
Summertime Cupcakes
Autumnal Cupcakes to Fall for
Winter Warmers
Holidays—Celebrate with Cupcakes

Meet the Sweet Treats! Each with a personality all its own, cupcakes are great for different events and an array of tastes. In this section, you'll find simple instructions for assembling scrumptious cakes, fabulous frostings, and sensational fillings from their relative chapters, and adding festive toppers to create perfect, little temptations. From the classically chic Sweet Cake to the adventurous Chocolate Pomegranate, you're bound to meet your cupcake soulmate.

Perennial Favorites

The Sweet Cake
Dark Chocolate
Karat
Cappuccino
Red Velvet
Boston Cream Pie
Vegan Chocolate
Pupcake

These classic flavors never take a vacation! Although many dessert aficionados fall into two very clear categories, vanilla and chocolate, *Sweet* has expanded the staple category to include one of their local heroes, the Boston Cream Pie, as well as a southern tradition, the Red Velvet. The classics are perfect and delectable basics suitable for children and adults of all ages! There's even one for our canine friends!

SWEET CAKE

Makes 12 cupcakes

These fluffy cupcakes are simple and elegant, yet versatile—a classic for all occasions! A white cake by design, the rich taste of vanilla shines through.

COMPONENTS

- Sweet Vanilla Cupcakes *(page 182)*
- Vanilla Buttercream Frosting *(page 203)*
- Pastry bag and tip, or knife
- Fondant and rubber stamp *(optional)*

DIRECTIONS

1. Prepare the Sweet Vanilla Cupcakes as directed and let cool.

2. As the cupcakes cool, prepare the Vanilla Buttercream Frosting. It should be freshly mixed and at room temperature at the time of decorating.

3. If piping the frosting *(see pages 123-25)*, make a small cut to the tip of the pastry bag with scissors. Insert the tip into the bag. Flip the top half of the pastry bag inside out, and use a spatula to fill it with the frosting. Squeeze some of the frosting out to rid the bag of any air pockets, and frost the cupcakes or spread the frosting on with a knife.

4. We've topped our Sweet Cake here with our signature "Sweet" stamped topper. To achieve this mod look, cut quarter-sized circles out of rolled

fondant and stamp in the center with your choice of a food-safe rubber stamp. You can also serve this classic alone or top with one of your favorite candies, or sliced fresh fruit. There are also many options for cake toppers available at decorating shops and online. You're sure to find one to match any theme you desire.

DARK CHOCOLATE
Makes 12 cupcakes

Flecks of rich chocolate throughout make this a favorite among true chocoholics and classic cake lovers alike.

COMPONENTS
- Dark Chocolate Cupcakes *(page 162)*
- Chocolate Buttercream Frosting *(page 190)*
- Pastry bag and tip, or knife
- Fondant and food stamp *(optional)*

DIRECTIONS
1. Prepare the Dark Chocolate Cupcakes as directed and let cool.

2. As the cupcakes cool, prepare the Chocolate Buttercream Frosting. It should be freshly mixed and at room temperature at the time of decorating.

3. If piping the frosting *(see pages 123-25)*, make a small cut to the tip of the pastry bag with scissors. Insert the tip into the bag. Flip the top half of the pastry bag inside out, and use a spatula to fill it with the frosting. Squeeze some of the frosting out to rid the bag of any air pockets, and frost the cupcakes or spread the frosting on with a knife.

4. We've topped our Dark Chocolate here with our signature "Sweet" stamped topper. To achieve this sharp look, cut quarter-sized circles out of rolled fondant and stamp in the center with your choice of

a food-safe rubber stamp. You can also serve this classic alone or top with one of your favorite candies. There are also many options for cake toppers available at decorating shops and online. You're sure to find one to match any theme you desire.

KARAT

Makes 12 cupcakes

This carrot cake is extra special, with chunks of fresh pineapple and a topper of edible gold. It's gilt without the guilt!

COMPONENTS
- Karat Cupcakes *(page 168)*
- Cream Cheese Frosting *(page 196)*
- Pastry bag and tip, or knife
- Edible gold leaf, or gold dragées (optional)

DIRECTIONS
1. Prepare the Karat Cupcakes as directed and let cool.

2. As the cupcakes cool, prepare the Cream Cheese Frosting. It should be freshly mixed and at room temperature at the time of decorating.

3. If piping the frosting *(see pages 123-25)*, make a small cut to the tip of the pastry bag with scissors. Insert the tip into the bag. Flip the top half of the pastry bag inside out, and use a spatula to fill it with the frosting. Squeeze some of the frosting out to rid the bag of any air pockets, and frost the cupcakes or spread the frosting on with a knife.

4. We've topped our Karat here with a fancy, edible gold leaf. You simply take a pinch of the edible gold and place atop each cupcake.

CAPPUCCINO

Makes 12 cupcakes

Based on the essential Italian espresso drink, this flavor consists of a rich, dense cake and is sure to wake you up or perfectly complement your after-dinner coffee.

COMPONENTS
- Cappuccino Cupcakes (*page 158*)
- Cappuccino Frosting (*page 188*)
- Pastry bag and tip, or knife
- Cinnamon (optional)

DIRECTIONS

1. Prepare the Cappuccino Cupcakes as directed and let cool.

2. As the cupcakes cool, prepare the Cappuccino Frosting. It should be freshly mixed and at room temperature at the time of decorating.

3. If piping the frosting (*see pages 123-25*), make a small cut to the tip of the pastry bag with scissors. Insert the tip into the bag. Flip the top half of the pastry bag inside out, and use a spatula to fill it with the frosting. Squeeze some of the frosting out to rid the bag of any air pockets, and frost the cupcakes or spread the frosting on with a knife.

4. Dust the tops evenly with cinnamon.

RED VELVET

Makes 12 cupcakes

In the southern tradition, this cocoa based cupcake is crimson through and through, in distinct contrast to its smooth white cream cheese frosting. Falling somewhere between vanilla and chocolate in flavor, this is a well-balanced dessert that is always the southern belle of the ball.

COMPONENTS
- Red Velvet Cupcakes *(page 178)*
- Cream Cheese Frosting *(page 196)*
- Pastry bag and tip, or knife
- 12 Chocolate Curls (optional)*

*Available at specialty shops, or you can make your own by shaving a chocolate block yourself!

DIRECTIONS
1. Prepare the Red Velvet Cupcakes as directed and let cool.

2. As the cupcakes cool, prepare the Cream Cheese Frosting. It should be freshly mixed and at room temperature at the time of decorating.

3. If piping the frosting *(see pages 123-25)*, make a small cut to the tip of the pastry bag with scissors. Insert the tip into the bag. Flip the top half of the pastry bag inside out, and use a spatula to fill it with

the frosting. Squeeze some of the frosting out to rid the bag of any air pockets, and frost the cupcakes or spread the frosting on with a knife.

4. Place a single chocolate curl on top of each for a touch of class.

BOSTON CREAM PIE

Makes 12 cupcakes

Delectable, light chiffon cake filled with homemade pastry cream and topped with a rich chocolate ganache make this Boston treat a hometown favorite. At Sweet, we use a fondant "cherry" to top it off, but you can also use fresh fruit or maraschino cherries!

COMPONENTS

- Pastry Cream Filling *(page 218)*
- Chiffon Cupcakes *(page 160)*
- Chocolate Ganache Frosting *(page 191)*
- Pastry bag and small round tip
- 12 Maraschino cherries (optional)

DIRECTIONS

1. Prepare the Pastry Cream Filling and let cool in the refrigerator for at least 3 hours.

2. Prepare the Chiffon Cupcakes as directed and let cool.

3. Make a small cut to the tip of the pastry bag with scissors. Insert the small round pastry tip into the bag. Once the Pastry Cream Filling is cooled, flip the top half of the pastry bag inside out, and use a spatula to fill it with the pastry cream. Squeeze some of the cream out to rid the bag of any air pockets.

4. Insert the tip just under the surface of the center of the chiffon cupcake and squeeze about one table-spoon of pastry cream directly into each cupcake. Because the cake is spongy, it will hold the cream perfectly in the center.

5. Prepare the Chocolate Ganache Frosting. When the ganache is still warm, but not hot, dip the al-ready-filled cupcakes one at a time, top down, into the chocolate ganache to coat, covering the wrapper just barely and shaking off the excess.

6. Once the chocolate ganache cools, garnish with a fresh, or maraschino, cherry. You can also make a cherry topper out of red and green fondant like we've done here.

VEGAN CHOCOLATE
Makes 12 cupcakes

This animal-product-free option is rich and luscious!

COMPONENTS
- Vegan Chocolate Cupcakes *(page 184)*
- Vegan Chocolate Frosting *(page 204)*
- Pastry bag and tip, or knife

DIRECTIONS
1. Prepare the Vegan Chocolate Cupcakes as directed and let cool.

2. As the cupcakes cool, prepare the Vegan Chocolate Frosting. It should be freshly mixed and at room temperature at the time of decorating.

3. If piping the frosting *(see pages 123-25)*, make a small cut to the tip of the pastry bag with scissors. Insert the tip into the bag. Flip the top half of the pastry bag inside out, and use a spatula to fill it with the frosting. Squeeze some of the frosting out to rid the bag of any air pockets, and frost the cupcakes or spread the frosting on with a knife.

4. We've left our Vegan Chocolate here simple and un-decorated, but there is a wide variety of candies that make fun, vegan toppers. (Note: make sure your candies are vegan—check to make sure they do not contain gelatin or carmine, which are animal-based ingredients).

PUPCAKE

Makes 24 mini pupcakes

A treat for man's best friend. See Spot run for the kitchen!

1¼ cups rolled oats
1 cup buttermilk
2 teaspoons ground cinnamon
1 teaspoon ground ginger
1 large egg
¼ cup honey
½ cup unsalted butter, melted
⅓ cup brown sugar, firmly-packed
1 cup all-purpose flour
1 teaspoon baking powder
½ teaspoon baking soda

1. Preheat the oven to 350°F.

2. Combine the oats, buttermilk, and spices in a large bowl and let the mixture stand for one-half to 1 hour.

3. Meanwhile, line 24 mini-muffin tin cups with mini cupcake paper liners.

4. Add all of the remaining ingredients to the oat mixture and mix until thoroughly combined.

5. Using a regular spoon, scoop the batter into the muffin tins, distributing evenly.

6. Bake until firm and golden brown (approximately 20 minutes).

Spring Cupcakes in Bloom

Chocolate Rhubarb
Chocolate Caramel
Lemon
Chocolate Coconut
Flourless Chocolate

Spring cupcakes are in bloom! Plant a garden of fresh flavors in these mouth-watering cupcakes. From Chocolate Rhubarb to tart Lemon, you're sure to find a cupcake that's ready to blossom in your kitchen for you, your friends, and family.

CHOCOLATE RHUBARB
Makes 12 cupcakes

What's sweet and tart, and oh so smart? A favorite pie ingredient, the glorious rhubarb sneaks its way into this luscious chocolate cupcake, topped with chocolate frosting.

COMPONENTS
- Rhubarb Preserves *(page 223)*
- Dark Chocolate Cupcakes *(page 162)*
- Chocolate Buttercream Frosting *(page 190)*
- 2 pastry bags and tip, or knife
- Strawberries, sliced (optional)

DIRECTIONS
1. Prepare the Rhubarb Preserves and let cool in the refrigerator.

2. Prepare the Dark Chocolate Cupcakes as directed and let cool.

3. Once the preserves are cool, make a small cut to the tip of a pastry bag with scissors. Flip the top half of the bag inside out, and use a spatula to fill it with the preserves. Squeeze some of the preserves out to rid the bag of any air pockets.

4. Using a teaspoon or apple corer, make a hole in the center of the top of each cupcake, being careful not to push the spoon or corer through the bottom of the cake.

5. Squeeze about one tablespoon of the preserves to fill the hole you've made in each cupcake.

6. Prepare the Chocolate Buttercream Frosting. It should be freshly mixed and at room temperature at the time of decorating.

7. If piping the frosting *(see pages 123-25)*, make a small cut to the tip of the second pastry bag with scissors. Insert the tip into the bag. Flip the top half of the pastry bag inside out, and use a spatula to fill it with the frosting. Squeeze some of the frosting out to rid the bag of any air pockets, and frost the cupcakes or spread the frosting on with a knife.

8. Top this rhubarb delight with a fresh strawberry sliver!

CHOCOLATE CARAMEL

Makes 12 cupcakes

A twist on the classic chocolate, this cupcake will spring you right into happiness, drizzled with gooey, yummy, caramel.

COMPONENTS

- Dark Chocolate Cupcakes *(page 162)*
- 1½ batches Chocolate Buttercream frosting, divided *(page 190)*
- 2 pastry bags and tip, or knife
- Caramel sauce (optional)

DIRECTIONS

1. Prepare the Dark Chocolate Cupcakes as directed and let cool.

2. Prepare the Chocolate Buttercream Frosting. It should be freshly mixed and at room temperature at the time of decorating.

3. Make a small cut to the tip of a pastry bag with scissors. Flip the top half of the bag inside out, and use a spatula to fill it with about ⅓ of the frosting. Squeeze some of the frosting out to rid the bag of any air pockets.

4. Using a teaspoon or apple corer, make a hole in the center of the top of each cupcake, being careful not to push the spoon or corer through the bottom of the cake.

5. Squeeze about one tablespoon of the frosting to fill the hole you've made in each cupcake.

6. If piping the frosting *(see pages 123-25)*, make a small cut to the tip of the second pastry bag with scissors. Insert the tip into the bag. Flip the top half of the pastry bag inside out, and use a spatula to fill it with the frosting. Squeeze some of the frosting out to rid the bag of any air pockets, and frost the cupcakes or spread the frosting on with a knife.

7. Warm the caramel sauce and drizzle over the tops of the cupcakes.

LEMON
Makes 12 cupcakes

Pucker up! This citrus-kissed variety is tart and sweet, a delight on fresh spring days.

COMPONENTS
- Lemon Cupcakes *(page 169)*
- Lemon Buttercream Frosting *(page 199)*
- Pastry bag and tip, or knife
- Candied lemon (optional)

DIRECTIONS
1. Prepare the Lemon Cupcakes as directed and let cool.

2. As the cupcakes cool, prepare the Lemon Buttercream Frosting. It should be freshly mixed and at room temperature at the time of decorating.

3. If piping the frosting *(see pages 123-25)*, make a small cut to the tip of the pastry bag with scissors. Insert the tip into the bag. Flip the top half of the pastry bag inside out, and use a spatula to fill it with the frosting. Squeeze some of the frosting out to rid the bag of any air pockets, and frost the cupcakes or spread the frosting on with a knife.

4. We've topped our Lemon cupcake here with a knotted piece of candied lemon. You could also use precious lemon candy dots, yellow dragées, or sliced lemon gummies as tart toppers.

CHOCOLATE COCONUT

Makes 12 cupcakes

Coconut is perfect in any season . . . and what better way to complement it than with a chocolate cupcake topped with a coconut cloud? Can someone say sweet dreams?

COMPONENTS

- Dark Chocolate Cupcakes *(page 162)*
- Coconut Buttercream Frosting *(page 193)*
- Pastry bag and tip, or knife
- Coconut shavings (optional)

DIRECTIONS

1. Prepare the Dark Chocolate Cupcakes as directed and let cool.

2. As the cupcakes cool, prepare the Coconut Buttercream Frosting. It should be freshly mixed and at room temperature at the time of decorating.

3. If piping the frosting *(see pages 123-25)*, make a small cut to the tip of the pastry bag with scissors. Insert the tip into the bag. Flip the top half of the pastry bag inside out, and use a spatula to fill it with the frosting. Squeeze some of the frosting out to rid the bag of any air pockets, and frost the cupcakes or spread the frosting on with a knife.

4. Sprinkle the tops or roll the frosted cupcakes in coconut shavings.

FLOURLESS CHOCOLATE

Makes 18 cupcakes

So rich, dense and delectable—you won't even need frosting for this flourless piece of heaven.

COMPONENTS
- Flourless Chocolate Cupcakes *(page 164)*
- Confectioners sugar (for dusting)

DIRECTIONS
1. Prepare the Flourless Chocolate Cupcakes as directed and let cool.

2. Dust the tops with confectioners sugar.

Summertime Cupcakes

Lemon Raspberry
Piña Colada
Red, White, and You
Strawberry Shortcake

From homemade whipping cream to ripe berries, the following flavors are wonderful summer options, whether you're pool-side or roof-top. Take shade underneath the tropical umbrella of a Piña Colada cupcake, or set some flavorful fireworks off with the delectable Red, White, and You cupcake sensation!

LEMON RASPBERRY

Makes 12 cupcakes

A simple spin on the lemon favorite, this one oozes with a taste straight from the berry bush.

COMPONENTS
- Raspberry Preserves *(page 222)*
- Lemon Cupcakes *(page 169)*
- Lemon Buttercream Frosting *(page 199)*
- 2 pastry bags and tip, or knife
- 12 fresh, ripe raspberries (optional)

DIRECTIONS
1. Prepare the Raspberry Preserves and let cool in the refrigerator.

2. Prepare the Lemon Cupcakes as directed and let cool.

3. Once the preserves are cool, make a small cut to the tip of a pastry bag with scissors. Flip the top half of the bag inside out, and use a spatula to fill it with the preserves. Squeeze some of the preserves out to rid the bag of any air pockets.

4. Using a teaspoon or apple corer, make a hole in the center of the top of each cupcake, being careful not to push the spoon or corer through the bottom of the cake.

5. Squeeze about one tablespoon of preserves to fill the hole you've made in each cupcake.

6. Prepare the Lemon Buttercream Frosting. It should be freshly mixed and at room temperature at the time of decorating.

7. If piping the frosting *(see pages 123-25)*, make a small cut to the tip of the second pastry bag with scissors. Insert the tip into the bag. Flip the top half of the pastry bag inside out, and use a spatula to fill it with the frosting. Squeeze some of the frosting out to rid the bag of any air pockets, and frost the cupcakes or spread the frosting on with a knife.

8. We've topped our Lemon Raspberry here with a juicy raspberry!

PIÑA COLADA
Makes 12 cupcakes

You'll love this virgin cupcake version of the tropical cocktail. Topped off with mini paper parasols, they are a real crowd pleaser!

COMPONENTS
- Pineapple Preserves *(page 220)*
- Sweet Vanilla Cupcakes *(page 182)*
- Coconut Buttercream Frosting *(page 193)*
- 2 pastry bags and tip, or knife
- 12 cocktail umbrellas (optional)

DIRECTIONS
1. Prepare the Pineapple Preserves and let cool in the refrigerator.

2. Prepare the Sweet Vanilla Cupcakes as directed and let cool.

3. Once the preserves are cool, make a small cut to the tip of a pastry bag with scissors. Flip the top half of the bag inside out, and use a spatula to fill it with the preserves. Squeeze some of the preserves out to rid the bag of any air pockets.

4. Using a teaspoon or apple corer, make a hole in the center of the top of each cupcake, being careful not to push the spoon or corer through the bottom of the cake.

5. Squeeze about one tablespoon of preserves to fill the hole you've made in each cupcake.

6. Prepare the Coconut Buttercream Frosting. It should be freshly mixed and at room temperature at the time of decorating.

7. If piping the frosting *(see pages 123-25)*, make a small cut to the tip of the second pastry bag with scissors. Insert the tip into the bag. Flip the top half of the pastry bag inside out, and use a spatula to fill it with the frosting. Squeeze some of the frosting out to rid the bag of any air pockets, and frost the cupcakes or spread the frosting on with a knife.

8. Top with a festive cocktail umbrella, like its sunny-day cocktail counterpart.

RED, WHITE, AND YOU

Makes 12 cupcakes

These are the sweetest Yankee Doodles you'll find—with a berry bash jam center that will make fireworks at your next patriotic BBQ.

COMPONENTS
- Berry Bash Jam *(page 210)*
- Sweet Vanilla Cupcakes *(page 182)*
- Vanilla Buttercream Frosting *(page 203)*
- 2 pastry bags and tip, or knife
- Red sanding sugar (optional)

DIRECTIONS
1. Prepare the Berry Bash Jam and let cool in the refrigerator.

2. Prepare the Sweet Vanilla Cupcakes as directed and let cool.

3. Once the jam is cool, make a small cut to the tip of a pastry bag with scissors. Flip the top half of the bag inside out, and use a spatula to fill it with the jam. Squeeze some of the jam out to rid the bag of any air pockets.

4. Using a teaspoon or apple corer, make a hole in the center of the top of each cupcake, being careful not to push the spoon or corer through the bottom of the cake.

5. Squeeze about one tablespoon of jam to fill the hole you've made in each cupcake.

6. Prepare the Vanilla Buttercream Frosting. It should be freshly mixed and at room temperature at the time of decorating.

7. If piping the frosting *(see pages 123-25)*, make a small cut to the tip of the second pastry bag with scissors. Insert the tip into the bag. Flip the top half of the pastry bag inside out, and use a spatula to fill it with the frosting. Squeeze some of the frosting out to rid the bag of any air pockets, and frost the cupcakes or spread the frosting on with a knife.

8. Sprinkle red sanding sugar onto a plate and roll the frosted cupcakes until evenly covered with a red sparkle!

STRAWBERRY SHORTCAKE

Makes 12 cupcakes

A summertime classic! Strawberry shortcake conjures
up cheerful images of sunny days under a shady tree.
Delectable vanilla cake and fresh strawberries are the
keys to this special summertime flavor.

COMPONENTS
* Strawberry Preserves *(page 224)*
* Sweet Vanilla Cupcakes *(page 182)*
* Whipped Cream Frosting *(page 205)*
* 2 pastry bags and tip, or knife
* Fresh strawberries (optional)

DIRECTIONS

1. Prepare the Strawberry Preserves and let cool in
   the refrigerator.

2. Prepare the Sweet Vanilla Cupcakes as directed
   and let cool.

3. Once the preserves are cool, make a small cut to the
   tip of a pastry bag with scissors. Flip the top half of
   the bag inside out, and use a spatula to fill it with
   the preserves. Squeeze some of the preserves out to
   rid the bag of any air pockets.

4. Using a teaspoon or apple corer, make a hole in the
   center of the top of each cupcake, being careful not
   to push the spoon or corer through the bottom of
   the cake.

5. Squeeze about one tablespoon of preserves to fill the hole you've made in each cupcake.

6. Prepare the Whipped Cream Frosting. It should be freshly mixed and at room temperature at the time of decorating.

7. If piping the frosting *(see pages 123-25)*, make a small cut to the tip of the second pastry bag with scissors. Insert the tip into the bag. Flip the top half of the pastry bag inside out, and use a spatula to fill it with the frosting. Squeeze some of the frosting out to rid the bag of any air pockets, and frost the cupcakes or spread the frosting on with a knife.

8. Slice several strawberries into small slivers and top each cupcake with a strawberry bite.

Autumnal Cupcakes to Fall for

Pumpkin
Brownie
Chocolate Cranberry
Caramel Apple
Molasses Ginger

School is back in session and the landscape changes from green to mottled reds and yellows. The bountiful harvest season offers leaf-piles of seasonal fruits and spices, and it's time to "reap" the benefits. Perfect for spooking trick-or-treaters, or on your Thanksgiving table, these flavors will make you feel at home, sweet home.

PUMPKIN
Makes 12 cupcakes

Enjoy this seasonal favorite in early autumn, while carving your Jack-o'-lantern's grin.

COMPONENTS
- Pumpkin Cupcakes *(page 176)*
- Cream Cheese Frosting *(page 196)*
- Pastry bag and tip, or knife
- 12 Cinnamon sugar pumpkin seeds (optional)

DIRECTIONS
1. Prepare the Pumpkin Cupcakes as directed and let cool.

2. As the cupcakes cool, prepare the Cream Cheese Frosting. It should be freshly mixed and at room temperature at the time of decorating.

3. If piping the frosting *(see pages 123-25)*, make a small cut to the tip of the pastry bag with scissors. Insert the tip into the bag. Flip the top half of the pastry bag inside out, and use a spatula to fill it with the frosting. Squeeze some of the frosting out to rid the bag of any air pockets, and frost the cupcakes or spread the frosting on with a knife.

4. Top each cupcake with a single cinnamon sugar pumpkin seed.

BROWNIE

Makes 12 cupcakes

This dense and fudgy chocolate cupcake is great when sitting by a fire, washed down with a nice cold glass of milk.

COMPONENTS
- Brownie Cupcakes *(page 155)*
- Chocolate Buttercream Frosting *(page 190)*
- Pastry bag and tip, or knife
- Caramel sauce (optional)
- Sea salt (optional)

DIRECTIONS
1. Prepare the Brownie Cupcakes as directed and let cool.

2. As the cupcakes cool, prepare the Chocolate Buttercream Frosting. It should be freshly mixed and at room temperature at the time of decorating.

3. If piping the frosting *(see pages 123-25)*, make a small cut to the tip of the pastry bag with scissors. Insert the tip into the bag. Flip the top half of the pastry bag inside out, and use a spatula to fill it with the frosting. Squeeze some of the frosting out to rid the bag of any air pockets, and frost the cupcakes or spread the frosting on with a knife.

4. Serve this double chocolate delight as is, or drizzle the tops with caramel sauce for a turtle treat. You can also omit the frosting altogether and sprinkle with flakes of sea salt for a sweet and salty flavor.

CHOCOLATE CRANBERRY

Makes 12 cupcakes

The fresh, tart cranberry filling, coupled with rich dark chocolate cake, makes this fall favorite irresistible.

COMPONENTS
- Cranberry Preserves *(page 215)*
- Dark Chocolate Cupcakes *(page 162)*
- Vanilla Buttercream Frosting *(page 203)*
- 2 pastry bags and tip, or knife
- Chocolate syrup (optional)
- 12 Chocolate-covered cranberries (optional)

DIRECTIONS
1. Prepare the Cranberry Preserves and let cool in the refrigerator.

2. Prepare the Dark Chocolate Cupcakes as directed and let cool.

3. Once the preserves are cool, make a small cut to the tip of a pastry bag with scissors. Flip the top half of the bag inside out, and use a spatula to fill it with the preserves. Squeeze some of the preserves out to rid the bag of any air pockets.

4. Using a teaspoon or apple corer, make a hole in the center of the top of each cupcake, being careful not to push the spoon or corer through the bottom of the cake.

5. Squeeze about one tablespoon of preserves to fill the hole you've made in each cupcake.

6. Prepare the Vanilla Buttercream Frosting. It should be freshly mixed and at room temperature at the time of decorating.

7. If piping the frosting *(see pages 123-25)*, make a small cut to the tip of the second pastry bag with scissors. Insert the tip into the bag. Flip the top half of the pastry bag inside out, and use a spatula to fill it with the frosting. Squeeze some of the frosting out to rid the bag of any air pockets, and frost the cupcakes or spread the frosting on with a knife.

8. Drizzle the tops with chocolate syrup and garnish with a chocolate-covered cranberry!

CARAMEL APPLE

Makes 12 cupcakes

With a taste straight from the county fair, it's a carnival of fall flavors complete with its own stick!

COMPONENTS
- Cinnamon Apple Preserves *(page 212)*
- Sweet Vanilla Cupcakes *(page 182)*
- Caramel Buttercream Frosting *(page 189)*
- 2 pastry bags and tip, or knife
- Caramel sauce, melted (optional)
- 12 Popsicle sticks (optional)

DIRECTIONS
1. Prepare the Cinnamon Apple Preserves and let cool in the refrigerator.

2. Prepare the Sweet Vanilla Cupcakes as directed and let cool.

3. Once the preserves are cool, make a small cut to the tip of a pastry bag with scissors. Flip the top half of the bag inside out, and use a spatula to fill it with the preserves. Squeeze some of the preserves out to rid the bag of any air pockets.

4. Using a teaspoon or apple corer, make a hole in the center of the top of each cupcake, being careful not to push the spoon or corer through the bottom of the cake.

5. Squeeze about one tablespoon of preserves to fill the hole you've made in each cupcake.

6. Prepare the Caramel Buttercream Frosting. It should be freshly mixed and at room temperature at the time of decorating.

7. If piping the frosting *(see pages 123-25)*, make a small cut to the tip of the second pastry bag with scissors. Insert the tip into the bag. Flip the top half of the pastry bag inside out, and use a spatula to fill it with the frosting. Squeeze some of the frosting out to rid the bag of any air pockets, and frost the cupcakes or spread the frosting on with a knife.

8. Drizzle with gooey melted caramel. Just as at the fair, a single Popsicle stick inserted into the center of the cupcake transforms this into an upside-down portable goody.

MOLASSES GINGER

Makes 12 cupcakes

A rich, spicy comfort when fall is coming to a close and you can feel the chill of winter creeping closer. This cupcake is great with a mug of mulled cider.

COMPONENTS
- Molasses Cupcakes *(page 172)*
- Ginger Buttercream Frosting *(page 197)*
- Pastry bag and tip, or knife
- Crystallized sugar (optional)

DIRECTIONS
1. Prepare the Molasses Cupcakes as directed and let cool.

2. As the cupcakes cool, prepare the Ginger Buttercream Frosting. It should be freshly mixed and at room temperature at the time of decorating.

3. If piping the frosting *(see pages 123-25)*, make a small cut to the tip of the pastry bag with scissors. Insert the tip into the bag. Flip the top half of the pastry bag inside out, and use a spatula to fill it with the frosting. Squeeze some of the frosting out to rid the bag of any air pockets, and frost the cupcakes or spread the frosting on with a knife.

4. Roll the frosted cupcakes lightly in a plate or bowl of crystallized sugar, or lightly sprinkle the sugar on top.

Winter Warmers

Blueberry Buttermilk Pancake
Banana Cream
Mocha Mint Chip
Buttered Orange Cider
Key Lime
Cookies & Cream
Snickerdoodle
Macaroon

Make a sweet escape with flavors designed to fight the cold and conjure up visions of comfort and warmer environs. Inspired by classic cookies, tropical getaways, and cozy times at home, there's a cupcake for winter in any climate.

BLUEBERRY BUTTER-MILK PANCAKE

Makes 12 cupcakes

For so long, relaxing Sunday brunch has come up against a roadblock on the dessert highway. This cupcake is the ultimate comfort food for a crisp morning.

COMPONENTS
- Blueberry Preserves *(page 211)*
- Buttermilk Pancake Cupcakes *(page 156)*
- Maple Buttercream Frosting *(page 200)*
- 2 pastry bags and tip, or knife
- Fresh blueberries (optional)
- Maple syrup (optional)

DIRECTIONS
1. Prepare the Blueberry Preserves and let cool in the refrigerator.

2. Prepare the Buttermilk Pancake Cupcakes as directed and let cool.

3. Once the preserves are cool, make a small cut to the tip of a pastry bag with scissors. Flip the top half of the bag inside out, and use a spatula to fill it with the preserves. Squeeze some of the preserves out to rid the bag of any air pockets.

4. Using a teaspoon or apple corer, make a hole in the center of the top of each cupcake, being careful not

to push the spoon or corer through the bottom of the cake.

5. Squeeze about one tablespoon of preserves to fill the hole you've made in each cupcake.

6. Prepare the Maple Buttercream Frosting. It should be freshly mixed and at room temperature at the time of decorating.

7. If piping the frosting *(see pages 123-25)*, make a small cut to the tip of the second pastry bag with scissors. Insert the tip into the bag. Flip the top half of the pastry bag inside out, and use a spatula to fill it with the frosting. Squeeze some of the frosting out to rid the bag of any air pockets, and frost the cupcakes or spread the frosting on with a knife.

8. Top with a fresh blueberry and, if having dessert for breakfast isn't sweet enough, drizzle with genuine maple syrup!

BANANA CREAM

Makes 12 cupcakes

*We're not monkeying around with this one! The rich,
banana caramel cream filling in this cupcake will have
you swinging from the trees.*

COMPONENTS
- Banana Caramel Cream Filling *(page 208)*
- Dark Chocolate Cupcakes *(page 162)*
- Vanilla Buttercream Frosting *(page 203)*
- 2 pastry bags and tip, or knife
- 12 Banana chips (optional)

DIRECTIONS
1. Prepare the Banana Caramel Cream Filling and let
   cool in the refrigerator for at least 3 hours.

2. Prepare the Dark Chocolate Cupcakes as directed
   and let cool.

3. Once the cream filling is cool, make a small cut to
   the tip of a pastry bag with scissors. Flip the top half
   of the bag inside out, and use a spatula to fill it with
   the cream filling. Squeeze some of the filling out to
   rid the bag of any air pockets.

4. Using a teaspoon or apple corer, make a hole in the
   center of the top of each cupcake, being careful not
   to push the spoon or corer through the bottom of
   the cake.

5. Squeeze about one tablespoon of the cream filling to fill the hole you've made in each cupcake.

6. Prepare the Vanilla Buttercream Frosting. It should be freshly mixed and at room temperature at the time of decorating.

7. If piping the frosting *(see pages 123-25)*, make a small cut to the tip of the second pastry bag with scissors. Insert the tip into the bag. Flip the top half of the pastry bag inside out, and use a spatula to fill it with the frosting. Squeeze some of the frosting out to rid the bag of any air pockets, and frost the cupcakes or spread the frosting on with a knife.

8. Top each cupcake with a banana chip.

MOCHA MINT CHIP

Makes 12 cupcakes

A delicious contrast of crisp and fresh mint frosting atop rich espresso-flavored cake, topped off with crunchy chocolate chips

COMPONENTS
- Cappuccino Cupcakes *(page 158)*
- Green Mint Buttercream Frosting *(page 198)*
- Pastry bag and tip, or knife
- Chocolate chips or flakes (optional)

DIRECTIONS

1. Prepare the Cappuccino Cupcakes as directed and let cool.

2. As the cupcakes cool, prepare the Green Mint Buttercream Frosting. It should be freshly mixed and at room temperature at the time of decorating.

3. If piping the frosting *(see pages 123-25)*, make a small cut to the tip of the pastry bag with scissors. Insert the tip into the bag. Flip the top half of the pastry bag inside out, and use a spatula to fill it with the frosting. Squeeze some of the frosting out to rid the bag of any air pockets, and frost the cupcakes or spread the frosting on with a knife.

4. Top each cupcake with a few chocolate chips or shavings.

BUTTERED ORANGE CIDER

Makes 12 cupcakes

Spiced orange-flavored cake pairs perfectly with its companion orange frosting. Dusted with seasonal spices, these cupcakes will warm you from head to toe!

COMPONENTS

- Orange Cider Cupcakes *(page 174)*
- Orange Spice Buttercream Frosting *(page 201)*
- Pastry bag and tip, or knife
- Nutmeg (for dusting)
- Cloves (for dusting)
- Cinnamon (for dusting)

DIRECTIONS

1. Prepare the Orange Cider Cupcakes as directed and let cool.

2. As the cupcakes cool, prepare the Orange Spice Buttercream Frosting. It should be freshly mixed and at room temperature at the time of decorating.

3. If piping the frosting *(see pages 123-25)*, make a small cut to the tip of the pastry bag with scissors. Insert the tip into the bag. Flip the top half of the pastry bag inside out, and use a spatula to fill it with the frosting. Squeeze some of the frosting out to rid the bag of any air pockets, and frost the cupcakes or

spread the frosting on with a knife.

4. Dust evenly with a mixture of the spices to evoke the rich scent of a pot of warm cider.

KEY LIME

Makes 12 cupcakes

A taste of the Keys—whenever and wherever—the Key Lime cupcake is the sweetest escape.

COMPONENTS
- Key Lime Curd Filling *(page 216)*
- Sweet Vanilla Cupcakes *(page 182)*
- Whipped Cream Frosting *(page 205)*
- 2 pastry bags and tip, or knife
- Graham cracker crumbles (optional)

DIRECTIONS
1. Prepare the Key Lime Curd Filling and let cool in the refrigerator (about ½ hour).

2. Prepare the Sweet Vanilla Cupcakes as directed and let cool.

3. Once the filling is cool, make a small cut to the tip of a pastry bag with scissors. Flip the top half of the bag inside out, and use a spatula to fill it with the curd filling. Squeeze some of the filling out to rid the bag of any air pockets.

4. Using a teaspoon or apple corer, make a hole in the center of the top of each cupcake, being careful not to push the spoon or corer through the bottom of the cake.

5. Squeeze about one tablespoon of filling to fill the hole you've made in each cupcake.

6. Prepare the Whipped Cream Frosting. It should be freshly mixed and at room temperature at the time of decorating.

7. If piping the frosting *(see pages 123-25)*, make a small cut to the tip of the second pastry bag with scissors. Insert the tip into the bag. Flip the top half of the pastry bag inside out, and use a spatula to fill it with the frosting. Squeeze some of the frosting out to rid the bag of any air pockets, and frost the cupcakes or spread the frosting on with a knife.

8. Dust each cupcake evenly with graham cracker crumbles to complete the pie combination!

COOKIES & CREAM

Makes 12 cupcakes

The classic sandwich cookie in a cupcake. Dipping it in milk might be tricky!

COMPONENTS
- Sweet Vanilla Cupcakes *(page 182)*
- Cookie Buttercream Frosting *(page 194)*
- Pastry bag and tip, or knife
- Chocolate cookie crumbles (optional)

DIRECTIONS
1. Prepare the Sweet Vanilla Cupcakes as directed and let cool.

2. As the cupcakes cool, prepare the Cookie Buttercream Frosting. It should be freshly mixed and at room temperature at the time of decorating.

3. If piping the frosting *(see pages 123-25)*, make a small cut to the tip of the pastry bag with scissors. Insert the tip into the bag. Flip the top half of the pastry bag inside out, and use a spatula to fill it with the frosting. Squeeze some of the frosting out to rid the bag of any air pockets, and frost the cupcakes or spread the frosting on with a knife.

4. For the cookie monster in the household, sprinkle even more chocolate cookie crumbles atop the frosting.

SNICKERDOODLE

Makes 12 cupcakes

A cupcake salute to the famous cookie! The crystallized sugar provides an unexpected cookie-like crunch.

COMPONENTS
- Snickerdoodle Cupcakes *(page 180)*
- Cinnamon Buttercream Frosting *(page 192)*
- Pastry bag and tip, or knife
- Crystallized sugar (optional)

DIRECTIONS
1. Prepare the Snickerdoodle Cupcakes as directed and let cool.

2. As the cupcakes cool, prepare the Cinnamon Buttercream Frosting. It should be freshly mixed and at room temperature at the time of decorating.

3. If piping the frosting *(see pages 123-25)*, make a small cut to the tip of the pastry bag with scissors. Insert the tip into the bag. Flip the top half of the pastry bag inside out, and use a spatula to fill it with the frosting. Squeeze some of the frosting out to rid the bag of any air pockets, and frost the cupcakes or spread the frosting on with a knife.

4. Roll the frosted cupcakes lightly in a plate or bowl of crystallized sugar, or lightly sprinkle the sugar on top.

MACAROON

Makes 12 cupcakes

The traditionally French confection comes home. Our nut-free version of the chewy cookie is packed with coconut and coated in chocolate ganache.

COMPONENTS
- Macaroon cupcakes *(page 170)*
- Chocolate Ganache frosting *(page 191)*
- Coconut shavings (optional)

DIRECTIONS
1. Prepare the Macaroon Cupcakes as directed and let cool.

2. Prepare the Chocolate Ganache Frosting. When the ganache is still warm, but not hot, dip the cooled cupcakes one at a time, top down, into the chocolate ganache to coat, covering the wrapper just barely and shaking off the excess.

3. Once the ganache cools, you can decorate with fresh or toasted coconut shavings.

Holidays—Celebrate with Cupcakes

Gingerbread
Candy Cane
Chocolate Ganache
Chocolate Pomegranate
Chocolate Raspberry
Chocolate Mint
Pumpkin Ginger

During this cheerful season, giving is in good taste, and no one can say no to a fresh-baked cupcake. With wintry flavors that make spirits bright, the following cupcakes are great for holiday parties and family get-togethers, bringing everyone closer together at the most wonderful time of the year.

GINGERBREAD

Makes 12 cupcakes

A holiday tradition, spiced to perfection and perfectly paired with homemade whipped cream!

COMPONENTS
- Gingerbread Cupcakes *(page 166)*
- Whipped Cream Frosting *(page 205)*
- Pastry bag and tip, or knife
- 12 mini gingerbread men cookies (optional)

DIRECTIONS
1. Prepare the Gingerbread Cupcakes as directed and let cool.

2. Prepare the Whipped Cream Frosting. It should be freshly mixed and at room temperature at the time of decorating.

3. If piping the frosting *(see pages 123-25)*, make a small cut to the tip of the pastry bag with scissors. Insert the tip into the bag. Flip the top half of the pastry bag inside out, and use a spatula to fill it with the frosting. Squeeze some of the frosting out to rid the bag of any air pockets, and frost the cupcakes or spread the frosting on with a knife.

4. Bake your own mini gingerbread men or use gingerbread cookies from the grocery store to top these holiday treats!

CANDY CANE

Makes 12 cupcakes

One taste of these mouth-tingling peppermint cupcakes, and you'll truly be in the spirit.

COMPONENTS
- Dark Chocolate Cupcakes *(page 162)*
- Peppermint Buttercream Frosting *(page 202)*
- Pastry bag and tip, or knife
- Chocolate syrup (optional)
- Candy cane crumbles (optional)

DIRECTIONS
1. Prepare the Dark Chocolate Cupcakes as directed and let cool.

2. As the cupcakes cool, prepare the Peppermint Buttercream Frosting. It should be freshly mixed and at room temperature at the time of decorating.

3. If piping the frosting *(see pages 123-25)*, make a small cut to the tip of the pastry bag with scissors. Insert the tip into the bag. Flip the top half of the pastry bag inside out, and use a spatula to fill it with the frosting. Squeeze some of the frosting out to rid the bag of any air pockets, and frost the cupcakes or spread the frosting on with a knife.

4. Drizzle each cupcake with chocolate syrup. Then take out your holiday stress and crush up some candy canes to crumble over the top.

CHOCOLATE GANACHE

Makes 12 cupcakes

Decadence in a cupcake! Rich chocolate cake dipped in smooth, dark chocolate ganache, and topped off with a white chocolate curl

COMPONENTS
- Dark Chocolate Cupcakes *(page 162)*
- Chocolate Ganache Frosting *(page 191)*
- 12 White chocolate curls (optional)*

Available at specialty shops, or you can make your own by shaving a white chocolate block yourself!

DIRECTIONS
1. Prepare the Dark Chocolate Cupcakes as directed and let cool.

2. Prepare the Chocolate Ganache Frosting. When the ganache is still warm, but not hot, dip the cooled cupcakes one at a time, top down, into the chocolate ganache to coat, covering the wrapper just barely and shaking off the excess.

3. Once the ganache cools, top each cupcake with a white chocolate curl.

CHOCOLATE POMEGRANATE

Makes 12 cupcakes

This flavor is quite daring and should only be attempted in small groups of gastronomes. The pomegranate filling is a clever nod to the winter season.

COMPONENTS

- Pomegranate Preserves *(page 221)*
- Dark Chocolate Cupcakes *(page 162)*
- Chocolate Buttercream Frosting *(page 190)*
- 2 pastry bags and tip, or knife
- Pomegranate syrup (optional)*
- 12 pomegranate seeds (optional)

*Available in select specialty stores or online.

DIRECTIONS

1. Prepare the Pomegranate Preserves and let cool in the refrigerator.

2. Prepare the Dark Chocolate Cupcakes as directed and let cool.

3. Once the preserves are cool, make a small cut to the tip of a pastry bag with scissors. Flip the top half of the bag inside out, and use a spatula to fill it with the preserves. Squeeze some of the preserves out to rid the bag of any air pockets.

4. Using a teaspoon or apple corer, make a hole in the center of the top of each cupcake, being careful not to push the spoon or corer through the bottom of the cake.

5. Squeeze about one tablespoon of preserves to fill the hole you've made in each cupcake.

6. Prepare the Chocolate Buttercream Frosting. It should be freshly mixed and at room temperature at the time of decorating.

7. If piping the frosting (*see pages 123-25*), make a small cut to the tip of the second pastry bag with scissors. Insert the tip into the bag. Flip the top half of the pastry bag inside out, and use a spatula to fill it with the frosting. Squeeze some of the frosting out to rid the bag of any air pockets, and frost the cupcakes or spread the frosting on with a knife.

8. Drizzle with tart, red pomegranate syrup or top with a single juicy pomegranate seed!

CHOCOLATE RASPBERRY

Makes 12 cupcakes

Delightful raspberry jam infuses chocolate cake with holiday spirit!

COMPONENTS
- Raspberry Preserves *(page 222)*
- Dark Chocolate Cupcakes *(page 162)*
- Chocolate Buttercream Frosting *(page 190)*
- 2 pastry bags and tip, or knife
- 12 Fresh raspberries (optional)

DIRECTIONS
1. Prepare the Raspberry Preserves and let cool in the refrigerator.

2. Prepare the Dark Chocolate Cupcakes as directed and let cool.

3. Once the preserves are cool, make a small cut to the tip of a pastry bag with scissors. Flip the top half of the bag inside out, and use a spatula to fill it with the preserves. Squeeze some of the preserves out to rid the bag of any air pockets.

4. Using a teaspoon or apple corer, make a hole in the center of the top of each cupcake, being careful not to push the spoon or corer through the bottom of the cake.

5. Squeeze about one tablespoon of preserves to fill the hole you've made in each cupcake.

6. Prepare the Choclate Buttercream Frosting. It should be freshly mixed and at room temperature at the time of decorating.

7. If piping the frosting *(see pages 123-25)*, make a small cut to the tip of the second pastry bag with scissors. Insert the tip into the bag. Flip the top half of the pastry bag inside out, and use a spatula to fill it with the frosting. Squeeze some of the frosting out to rid the bag of any air pockets, and frost the cupcakes or spread the frosting on with a knife.

8. Top each cupcake with a ripe, luscious raspberry.

CHOCOLATE MINT
Makes 12 cupcakes

The classic combination of chocolate and mint feels particularly appropriate during this delicious, festive season.

COMPONENTS
- Dark Chocolate Cupcakes *(page 162)*
- Green Mint Buttercream Frosting *(page 198)*
- Pastry bag and tip, or knife
- Chocolate Shavings (optional)*

*Available at specialty shops, or you can make your own by shaving a chocolate block yourself!

DIRECTIONS
1. Prepare the Dark Chocolate cupcakes as directed and let cool.

2. As the cupcakes cool, prepare the Green Mint Buttercream Frosting. It should be freshly mixed and at room temperature at the time of decorating.

3. If piping the frosting *(see pages 123-25)*, make a small cut to the tip of the pastry bag with scissors. Insert the tip into the bag. Flip the top half of the pastry bag inside out, and use a spatula to fill it with the frosting. Squeeze some of the frosting out to rid the bag of any air pockets, and frost the cupcakes or spread the frosting on with a knife.

4. Top these with chocolate shavings to add whimsy to this pale green refresher.

PUMPKIN GINGER

Makes 12 cupcakes

Kick fall's pumpkin cake into winter with a shot of spicy ginger buttercream frosting!

COMPONENTS
- Pumpkin Cupcakes *(page 176)*
- Ginger Buttercream Frosting *(page 197)*
- Pastry bag and tip, or knife
- Crystallized sugar (optional)

DIRECTIONS
1. Prepare the Pumpkin Cupcakes as directed and let cool.

2. As the cupcakes cool, prepare the Ginger Buttercream Frosting. It should be freshly mixed and at room temperature at the time of decorating.

3. If piping the frosting *(see pages 123-25)*, make a small cut to the tip of the pastry bag with scissors. Insert the tip into the bag. Flip the top half of the pastry bag inside out, and use a spatula to fill it with the frosting. Squeeze some of the frosting out to rid the bag of any air pockets, and frost the cupcakes or spread the frosting on with a knife.

4. Roll the frosted cupcakes lightly in a plate or bowl of crystallized sugar, or lightly sprinkle the tops with sugar.

Decorating Ideas & Special Occasions

DECORATING IDEAS

Frost Like a Pro!

There are two basic methods for frosting cupcakes: knife-spreading and piping. The former requires only one tool—the knife, of course! This is the way you watched your mother and your grandmother frost cupcakes, so if traditional is your style, reach for the silverware drawer. Piping the frosting on the cupcakes with standard pastry bags and tips is a simple way to add whimsy to your creations. The proper tools can be found at your local bakery supply store or online: try *wilton.com* or *nycake.com* for a variety of bags, tips, and other cupcake decorating supplies. Piping is an art form that requires practice, but once you get the hang of it, you'll find that it can be a quick and easy way to create professional-looking results. That's the icing on the cake (excuse the pun)!

As far as pastry tips go, the rules are there are no rules; the number of the tip will go up with the size of the opening, so feel free to explore different tips for smaller and larger dollops. To decorate, the cupcakes need to be completely cool beforehand, and the frosting should be freshly mixed and at room temperature. Make a small cut to the tip of the pastry bag with scissors. Insert the tip into the pastry bag. Flip the top half of the bag inside out, use a spatula to fill it with the frosting about halfway to the top, and squeeze some frosting out to rid the bag of any air pockets. Then frost your heart out!

Here are some samples of frosting styles that you can create by using four basic pastry tips. Visit **www.bakeitpretty.com** to purchase a convenient kit that has all four tips, plus a pastry bag included.

For a dreamy cloud of frosting, use a large round tip. Hold the tip close to the top center of the cake, and squeeze the frosting out until it covers the cake. Then, lift the bag just slightly, and repeat for a smaller layer.

www.bakeitpretty.com

To create a classically swirled cupcake, use a large star tip. Start from the outer edge of the cupcake, swirl your way toward the center, and pull up for the center tip.

www.bakeitpretty.com

For a fluffier, ribbon-like frost, substitute a closed star tip for the regular star tip.

A popular style for the Francophile is created by decorating with the French tip. This makes a delicious-looking cupcake with many tiny-ridged swirls.

Tip-Toppings!

To make your cupcakes really stand out (and to help your guests know which cupcake is which flavor), there is a multitude of drizzles, crumbles, and other tasty additions for the top of your finished dessert. As shown in the first half of this little book, finishing touches are the key to creating the complete package—a delicious and gorgeous treat that begs to be eaten. The following are some of the ingredients we use to top our cupcakes. Don't be afraid to experiment!

- **Fruit**—fresh, chocolate-covered, candied, or dried
- **Sprinkles**—sanding sugar, nonpareils, dragées
- **Crumbles**—cookie, candy, crystallized sugar, graham cracker
- **Drizzles**—butterscotch, caramel, pomegranate, rhubarb, chocolate-flavored syrups*
- **Savory**—sea salt
- **Spices**—cinnamon, nutmeg, cloves
- **Chocolate delights**—chips, shavings, curls**
- **Specialty items**—shaped cookies (like gingerbread men), coconut shavings, cinnamon sugar, pumpkin seeds, and edible gold or silver leaf
- **Inedible**—cocktail straws and umbrellas, swizzle sticks

*A variety of flavored syrups can be found in specialty shops, or online. Try these:

www.dejondelights.com
www.davincigourmet.com
www.torani.com

**Decadent chocolate toppers can be found in specialty shops, or online. Try these:

> *www.chocolate.com*
> *www.choclatique.com*

If you don't have access to a baking supply store in your area, you can find lots of fun fixings online. From sparkling gold dust and sugar crystals in every color of the rainbow to premade edible flowers and confetti, you'll be sure to find inspiring toppings for any occasion! Check out these websites:

> *www.bakeitpretty.com*
> *www.globalsugarart.com*
> *www.shopbakersnook.com*
> *www.sugarcraft.com*

Make Your Own Toppings— Festive Fondant!

Fondant icing, or rolled fondant, is a dough-like edible sugary material that can be used to create your own shapes and designs. You can make your own fondant or buy it ready-made or as a powdered mix from a bakery supply store or online. It is available in a variety of colors and easy to work with, so coming up with fun fondant designs is no sweat! Roll the fondant out and flatten it with a rolling pin. Then cut shapes out with tiny cookie cutters, or stamp and emboss images into the fondant. You can mold the fondant like clay to create three-dimensional objects. Some helpful tools for fondant work are a paintbrush (to moisten the fondant to enhance the adhesiveness) and toothpicks (to assemble bodies and other composite shapes). Be sure to allow your fondant creations to dry thoroughly before serving.

Birthday!

Cupcakes are a fun and creative way to celebrate birthdays. Arrange them in the shape of the guest of honor's age or top with monograms, birthday messages, or spell out a sweet greeting!

You can find letter-shaped cut-outs online or you can simply cut a circle out of fondant and pipe the letters on in frosting with a very small round pastry tip.

KID'S BIRTHDAY

If you liked playing with clay when you were younger, these cupcakes will give you the chance to realize that childhood memory. Create special memories for a child's birthday by fashioning fondant into an adorable menagerie like pigs, ducks, monkeys, and ladybugs. If sculpting eludes you, purchase ready-made toppers online or revert to simpler designs.

Maybe you'd like to create a frosting perch for ladybugs, butterflies, and other spring creatures. Select a leaf decorating tip and squeeze the frosting out rapidly, so that it creates a wavy look. And then place your critter on top!

BABY SHOWER

For a touch of elegance at a baby shower, add
food dye to Vanilla Buttercream frosting for a
charming, subtle pastel scheme.

You can also cut baby shapes out of fondant,
like the baby carriage and bottle below, or shop
around for storks, teddy bears, and other cute
cookie-cutter shapes.

BRIDAL SHOWER

Impress the bride-to-be and her guests with a lovely tier of cupcakes. A little presentation goes a long way and you'll be amazed at all of the *oohs* and *ahhs* that a 3-tiered tower of sweetness can bring! Add food dye to the Vanilla Buttercream Frosting in light pastel shades, or you may want to use the bride's wedding colors as inspiration for decorating your cupcakes.

VALENTINE'S DAY

How about a sweet treat for your sweetheart? By rolling your first dollop of frosting in red sprinkles, then topping with the second dollop, you can recreate this flirty look to show your loved ones how much you care. Or use a heart-shaped cutter to make sweet heart toppers out of fondant as pictured below.

St. Patrick's Day!

Top o' the cupcake to ya! Like the Valentine's Day cupcakes *(page 141)*, you can roll these in assorted green sprinkles or go green by dying Vanilla Buttercream frosting in your luckiest shade. Try your hand at piping some shamrock designs by using a very small round pastry tip. Practice on wax paper first to try out a few designs before piping onto the cupcakes.

EASTER

Hop to it! You can cut chick and bunny shapes out of fondant or mold the fondant into bunnies, carrots, and more. Candy corn and a bevy of Easter candy make terrific toppers.

Or knife-frost your cupcake with a thin layer of dyed frosting and use chocolate shavings and mini chocolate eggs to create a little nest. Hatch your own ideas, too!

HALLOWEEN

Shape gray fondant into a gravestone, pipe on an RIP, and place on top of your Cookies & Cream cupcake *(see page 96)* for the tastiest graveyard this side of the wrought iron gate. Spiderwebs made of frosting are simply spine-tingling. With a small round tip, draw lines from the center outward, then connect with curved lines in a web pattern that'll catch your eye and the fly. Use the same small round tip and black frosting to pipe a spider in the center. Lastly, fondant cut out shapes are always an easy way to add trick to your treat. Ghost, bat, and pumpkin cutters can be found online.

CHRISTMAS

In addition to the delicious holiday favorites earlier in the book, add your own twinkle to the season with these special designs.

Roll out red fondant and use two different sized flower cutouts to create your flower shapes. After you've frosted the cupcake, layer the flower fondants on top. (If you're also using a leaf shape, apply that first.) Then top it off with a single silver dragée in the center, and green sprinkles. Feel free to experiment with whatever festive shape cutters you find. Rudolph and his reindeer make excellent toppers!

What says Merry Christmas more than a traditionally decorated tree? Insert a round large tip into a pastry bag. Fill the bag with green frosting. Hold the tip close to the top center of the cake and squeeze out the frosting to cover the cake, then lift the bag just slightly, and squeeze more frosting out for a second dollop. This will act as your base form for the tree. Then insert a small star tip into another pastry bag and fill it with more of the green frosting. Starting at the base, make small circular motions as you squeeze out the frosting onto the tree base. Work your way up and around until you have formed the tree. Top with festive dragées or sprinkles. If you want your tree to really shine, roll out yellow fondant and create stars using star cut outs. Gently place them on top, pushing them just slightly down into the frosting.

Sweet's Master Cupcake Recipes

Brownie Cupcakes
Buttermilk Pancake Cupcakes
Cappuccino Cupcakes
Chiffon Cupcakes
Dark Chocolate Cupcakes
Flourless Chocolate Cupcakes
Gingerbread Cupcakes
Karat Cupcakes
Lemon Cupcakes
Macaroon Cupcakes
Molasses Cupcakes
Orange Cider Cupcakes
Pumpkin Cupcakes
Red Velvet Cupcakes
Snickerdoodle (Cinnamon) Cupcakes
Sweet Vanilla Cupcakes
Vegan Chocolate Cupcakes

Now that you have the basics down, and you've met all the cupcakes, it's time for a cake walk through *Sweet's* master cupcake recipes! These cupcake recipes are the bread to your buttercream, the blank canvas on which to paint delicious tasting, and looking, pieces of art.

Brownie Cupcakes
Makes 12 cupcakes

¾ cup unsalted butter
3 ounces dark chocolate, chopped
1¼ cup sugar
1 tablespoon vanilla extract
2 large eggs
¾ cup all-purpose flour, sifted
½ cup cocoa powder, sifted
½ teaspoon salt

1. Preheat the oven to 350°F.

2. Line 12 muffin tin cups with paper cupcake liners.

3. In a double boiler, melt together the butter and chocolate over low heat.

4. In an electric mixer, or large bowl, add sugar and then mix in the melted chocolate mixture at high speed for approximately 4 to 5 minutes.

5. Add the vanilla and eggs and mix for 30 seconds.

6. Add the flour, cocoa powder, and salt, and blend.

7. Pour the batter into the lined cupcake pan, distributing the batter equally.

8. Bake for 12 minutes, rotate, and bake for 12 more minutes or until a toothpick inserted in the center of a cupcake comes out clean.

9. Place the pan on a wire rack, and cool completely.

Buttermilk Pancake Cupcakes
Makes 12 cupcakes

2 cups all-purpose flour
2 tablespoons sugar
2 teaspoons baking powder
1/2 teaspoon baking soda
1/2 teaspoon salt
2 1/2 tablespoons unsalted butter
1 large egg
2 cups buttermilk

1. Preheat the oven to 350°F.

2. Line 12 muffin tin cups with paper cupcake liners.

3. Sift the flour, sugar, baking powder, baking soda, and salt into a medium bowl.

4. In a small bowl, melt the butter in the microwave.

5. In a large mixing bowl, whisk together the egg, melted butter, and buttermilk until well blended.

6. Add the flour mixture to the buttermilk mixture and blend until fully incorporated.

7. Pour the batter into the lined cupcake pan, distributing the batter equally.

8. Bake for 5 minutes, rotate, and bake for 10 more minutes. Then rotate again and bake for 5 more minutes or until a toothpick inserted in the center of a cupcake comes out clean.

9. Place the pan on a wire rack, and cool completely.

Cappuccino Cupcakes
Makes 12 cupcakes

2 ounces unsweetened chocolate, chopped
1 cup cake flour
¾ teaspoon baking powder
½ teaspoon cinnamon
1 teaspoon espresso powder
¾ cup whole milk
¼ cup unsalted butter, room temperature
1 cup sugar
1 large egg
1 teaspoon vanilla extract

1. Preheat the oven to 350°F.

2. Line 12 muffin tin cups with paper cupcake liners.

3. Stir chocolate in a double boiler over low heat, until just melted. Remove from heat and set aside.

4. Sift flour, baking powder, and cinnamon into a medium bowl.

5. In a separate bowl, add the espresso powder to the milk to dissolve.

6. In an electric mixer, or large bowl, beat the butter and sugar until light and fluffy.

7. Beat in the egg until well blended.

8. Mix in the melted chocolate and the vanilla extract.

9. Add the milk mixture and flour mixture alter-

nately into the butter mixture on low speed, in four increments, ending with flour mixture. Beat until smooth.

10. Pour the batter into the lined cupcake pan, distributing the batter equally.

11. Bake for 10 minutes, rotate, and bake for 12 more minutes, or until a toothpick inserted in the center of a cupcake comes out clean.

12. Place the pan on a wire rack, and cool completely.

Chiffon Cupcakes
Makes 12 cupcakes

¾ cup sugar
1 cup cake flour
1 teaspoon baking powder
3 large eggs, divided
⅓ cup water
¼ cup canola oil
1½ teaspoons vanilla extract
¼ teaspoon cream of tartar

1. Preheat the oven to 350°F.

2. Line 12 muffin tin cups with paper cupcake liners.

3. In a medium bowl, mix the sugar, cake flour, and baking powder together.

4. Separate two of the egg whites and two of the egg yolks into two separate large bowls.

5. Add the third whole egg to the bowl with the egg yolks. Then add the water, oil, and vanilla and whisk until smooth.

6. Add the flour mixture to the egg and water mixture and blend until smooth.

7. With an electric mixer, beat the egg whites on medium speed until foamy.

8. Add the cream of tartar to the egg whites and beat on high speed until stiff.

9. Add the egg whites mixture to the other wet mixture, gently folding it in with a spatula until smooth.

10. Pour the batter into the lined cupcake pan, distributing the batter equally.

11. Bake for 10 minutes, rotate, and bake for 10 more minutes, or until a toothpick inserted in the center of a cupcake comes out clean.

12. Place the pan on a wire rack, and cool completely.

Dark Chocolate Cupcakes
Makes 12 cupcakes

1 cup cake flour
$^1/_2$ cup cocoa powder
$^1/_2$ teaspoon baking soda
$^1/_4$ teaspoon baking powder
1 ounce bittersweet chocolate, finely chopped
$^1/_2$ cup unsalted butter, room temperature
1 cup sugar
2 large eggs
2 teaspoons vanilla extract
$^3/_4$ cup buttermilk

1. Preheat the oven to 350°F.

2. Line 12 muffin tin cups with paper cupcake liners.

3. Sift the cake flour, cocoa powder, baking soda, and baking powder into a medium bowl. Mix in the bittersweet chocolate.

4. In an electric mixer, or large bowl, beat the butter and sugar until light and fluffy.

5. Beat in the eggs one at a time until well blended, and then beat in the vanilla extract.

6. Add the buttermilk to the butter mixture on low speed and blend well. Then add the flour mixture and beat until smooth.

7. Pour the batter into the lined cupcake pan, distributing the batter equally.

8. Bake for 8 minutes, then rotate, and bake for 8 more minutes, or until a toothpick inserted in the center of a cupcake comes out clean.

9. Place the pan on a wire rack, and cool completely.

Flourless Chocolate Cupcakes
Makes 18 cupcakes

12 ounces semi-sweet chocolate, chopped
¾ cup unsalted butter, room temperature, cut into pieces
6 large eggs, room temperature
12 tablespoons sugar, divided
2 teaspoons vanilla extract
1 teaspoon instant espresso

1. Preheat the oven to 350°F.

2. Line 18 muffin tin cups with paper cupcake liners.

3. Stir the chocolate and butter in a heavy, medium-sized saucepan over low heat until melted and smooth (stirring constantly). Remove from the heat and cool to lukewarm, stirring often. Set aside.

4. Separate the egg whites and egg yolks into two separate large bowls.

5. Add 6 tablespoons of the sugar to the egg yolks, and beat on medium to high speed, until the mixture is very thick and pale (about 3 minutes).

6. Fold the chocolate mixture into the egg yolk mixture with a spatula. Then fold in the vanilla extract and instant espresso.

7. Using clean and dry beaters, beat the egg whites in their separate bowl on high speed until soft peaks form.

8. Gradually add in the remaining 6 tablespoons of sugar, beating until medium-firm peaks form.

9. Fold the egg whites into the chocolate mixture in 3 batches with a spatula.

10. Pour the batter into the lined cupcake pan, distributing the batter equally.

11. Bake for 10 minutes, then rotate and bake for 12 more minutes.

12. Place the pan on a wire rack, and cool completely.

Gingerbread Cupcakes
Makes 12 cupcakes

1 cup all-purpose flour
1 teaspoon baking soda
1¼ teaspoons ginger
½ teaspoon cinnamon
¼ teaspoon ground cloves
⅔ cup hot water
⅔ cup molasses
⅓ cup unsalted butter, room temperature
⅓ cup sugar
2½ tablespoons egg beaters

1. Preheat the oven to 350°F.

2. Line 12 muffin tin cups with paper cupcake liners.

3. Sift the flour, baking soda, ginger, cinnamon, and cloves together in a medium bowl.

4. In a separate bowl, mix the hot water and molasses together.

5. In an electric mixer, or large bowl, beat the butter until light and fluffy, and then gradually add in the sugar and mix well.

6. Beat in the egg beaters until well blended.

7. Reduce speed to low, add flour mixture and molasses mixture alternately in three batches to the butter mixture, beginning and ending with flour. Beat gently until smooth.

8. Pour the batter into the lined cupcake pan, distributing the batter equally.

9. Bake for 8 minutes, rotate, and bake for 8 more minutes or until a toothpick inserted in the center of a cupcake comes out clean.

10. Place the pan on a wire rack, and cool completely.

Karat Cupcakes

Makes 12 cupcakes

1 cup all-purpose flour
$^1/_8$ teaspoon nutmeg
$^1/_8$ teaspoon ginger
$^3/_4$ teaspoon cinnamon
2 teaspoons baking soda
1 cup sugar
2 eggs
$^1/_4$ cup vegetable oil
$^1/_4$ cup drained canned pineapple, diced
1 cup carrots, peeled and diced

1. Preheat the oven to 325°F.

2. Line 12 muffin tin cups with paper cupcake liners.

3. Sift the flour, nutmeg, ginger, cinnamon, and baking soda into a medium bowl.

4. In an electric mixer, or large bowl, beat the sugar, eggs, and vegetable oil together until well blended.

5. Add the pineapple and carrots and mix well.

6. Add the flour mixture and beat on low speed.

7. Pour the batter into the lined cupcake pan, distributing the batter equally.

8. Bake for 10 minutes, rotate, and bake for 8 more minutes, or until a toothpick inserted in the center of a cupcake comes out clean.

9. Place the pan on a wire rack, and cool completely.

Lemon Cupcakes

Makes 12 cupcakes

1½ cups cake flour
1½ teaspoons baking powder
6 tablespoons unsalted butter, room temperature
¾ cup sugar
2 large eggs, room temperature
1 tablespoon lemon extract
½ cup, plus 2 tablespoons whole milk

1. Preheat the oven to 350°F.

2. Line 12 muffin tin cups with paper cupcake liners.

3. Sift the flour and baking powder into a medium bowl.

4. In an electric mixer, or large bowl, beat the butter and sugar, on medium speed, until light and fluffy.

5. Beat in the eggs one at a time, until well blended.

6. Beat in the lemon extract, blending well.

7. Reduce speed to low, add the milk and blend well. Then add the flour mixture and beat until smooth.

8. Pour the batter into the lined cupcake pan, distributing the batter equally.

9. Bake for 8 minutes, rotate, and bake for 7 more minutes or until a toothpick inserted in the center of a cupcake comes out clean.

10. Place the pan on a wire rack, and cool completely.

Macaroon Cupcakes

Makes 12 cupcakes

1⅔ cups cake flour
1⅛ teaspoons baking powder
¼ teaspoon salt
⅓ cup unsalted butter, room temperature
¾ cup, plus 2 tablespoons sugar
1 large egg
¾ cup whole milk
1⅛ teaspoon vanilla extract
½ cup shredded coconut

1. Preheat the oven to 320°F.

2. Line 12 muffin tin cups with paper cupcake liners.

3. Sift the flour, baking powder, and salt into a medium bowl.

4. In an electric mixer, or large bowl, beat the butter until light and fluffy, and then gradually add in the sugar and mix well.

5. Beat in the egg until well blended.

6. Measure the milk into a separate bowl and add the vanilla.

7. Reduce speed to low, and add the flour mixture and milk alternately in three steps to the butter mixture, beginning and ending with flour. Beat until smooth.

8. Add the coconut and mix for a few seconds.

9. Pour the batter into the lined cupcake pan, distributing the batter equally.

10. Bake for 8 minutes, rotate, and bake for 9 more minutes or until a toothpick inserted in the center of a cupcake comes out clean.

11. Place the pan on a wire rack, and cool completely.

Molasses Cupcakes
Makes 12 cupcakes

1²/₃ cups cake flour
1¹/₈ teaspoons baking powder
¹/₄ teaspoon salt
¹/₈ teaspoon ginger
1¹/₂ teaspoons cinnamon
¹/₂ teaspoon ground cloves
¹/₃ cup unsalted butter, room temperature
³/₄ cup, plus 2 tablespoons sugar
1 large egg
³/₄ cup whole milk
1¹/₈ teaspoons vanilla extract
¹/₃ cup molasses

1. Preheat the oven to 350°F.

2. Line 12 muffin tin cups with paper cupcake liners.

3. Sift flour, baking powder, salt, ginger, cinnamon, and cloves together in a medium bowl.

4. In an electric mixer, or large bowl, beat the butter until light and fluffy, and then gradually add in the sugar and mix well.

5. Beat in the egg until well blended.

6. Measure the milk into a separate bowl, add in the vanilla and set aside.

7. Add the molasses into the butter and sugar mixture and blend.

8. Reduce speed to low, add flour and milk alternately in three steps to the butter mixture, beginning and ending with flour. Beat gently until smooth.

9. Pour the batter into the lined cupcake pan, distributing the batter equally.

10. Bake for 10 minutes, rotate, and bake for 12 more minutes or until a toothpick inserted in the center of a cupcake comes out clean.

11. Place the pan on a wire rack, and cool completely.

Orange Cider Cupcakes
Makes 12 cupcakes

1$\frac{2}{3}$ cups cake flour
1$\frac{1}{8}$ teaspoons baking powder
1$\frac{1}{2}$ teaspoons cinnamon
$\frac{1}{2}$ teaspoon ground cloves
$\frac{1}{8}$ teaspoon nutmeg
$\frac{1}{4}$ teaspoon salt
$\frac{1}{3}$ cup unsalted butter, room temperature
$\frac{3}{4}$ cup, plus 2 tablespoons sugar
1 large egg
$\frac{3}{4}$ cup whole milk
1$\frac{1}{8}$ teaspoons vanilla extract
2$\frac{1}{2}$ teaspoons orange flavor

1. Preheat the oven to 300°F.

2. Line 12 muffin tin cups with paper cupcake liners.

3. Sift the flour, baking powder, cinnamon, cloves, nutmeg, and salt into a medium bowl.

4. In an electric mixer, or large bowl, beat the butter until light and fluffy, and then gradually add in the sugar and mix well.

5. Beat in the egg until well blended.

6. Measure the milk into a separate bowl and add the vanilla.

7. Reduce speed to low, and add the flour mixture and milk alternately in three steps to the butter

mixture, beginning and ending with flour and beat gently until smooth.

8. Add the orange flavor and mix until fully incorporated.

9. Pour the batter into the lined cupcake pan, distributing the batter equally.

10. Bake for 10 minutes, rotate, and bake for 12 more minutes or until a toothpick inserted in the center of a cupcake comes out clean.

11. Place the pan on a wire rack, and cool completely.

Pumpkin Cupcakes
Makes 12 cupcakes

1⅓ cups cake flour
1¼ teaspoons baking powder
½ teaspoon cinnamon
¼ teaspoon nutmeg
¼ teaspoon baking soda
⅛ teaspoon ground cloves
⅓ cup unsalted butter, room temperature
1 cup light brown sugar, firmly packed
1 large egg
⅓ cup, plus 1 tablespoon and 1 teaspoon whole milk
⅔ cup pumpkin

1. Preheat the oven to 350°F.

2. Line 12 muffin tin cups with paper cupcake liners.

3. Sift the flour, baking powder, cinnamon, nutmeg, baking soda, and cloves into a medium bowl.

4. In an electric mixer, or large bowl, beat the butter until light and fluffy, and then gradually add in the brown sugar and mix well.

5. Beat in the egg until well blended.

6. Add the milk to the butter mixture and blend well. Then add the flour mixture and beat until smooth.

7. Add the pumpkin and mix until smooth.

8. Pour the batter into the lined cupcake pan, distributing the batter equally.

9. Bake for 10 minutes, rotate, and bake for 17 more minutes or until a toothpick inserted in the center of a cupcake comes out clean.

10. Place the pan on a wire rack, and cool completely.

Red Velvet Cupcakes

Makes 12 cupcakes

¾ cup unsalted butter, room temperature
1 cup sugar
2 large eggs
2½ tablespoons red food coloring
1½ tablespoons cocoa powder
¾ cup buttermilk
1½ cups cake flour, sifted
1 teaspoon vinegar
¾ teaspoon baking soda

1. Preheat the oven to 350°F.

2. Line 12 muffin tin cups with paper cupcake liners.

3. In an electric mixer, or large bowl, beat the butter and sugar until light and fluffy.

4. Beat in the eggs one at a time, until well blended.

5. In a separate bowl, mix the food coloring and cocoa powder until you have a paste.

6. Add the paste to the butter mixture, and blend well.

7. Add the buttermilk to the butter mixture and blend well. Then add the flour and blend until smooth.

8. In a separate bowl, mix together the vinegar and baking soda. Then add this to the butter and flour mixture, blending until fully incorporated.

9. Pour the batter into the lined cupcake pan, distributing the batter equally.

10. Bake for 10 minutes, rotate, and bake for 10 more minutes or until a toothpick inserted in the center of a cupcake comes out clean.

11. Place the pan on a wire rack, and cool completely.

Snickerdoodle (Cinnamon) Cupcakes

Makes 12 cupcakes

1²/₃ cups cake flour
1¹/₈ teaspoons baking powder
4 teaspoons cinnamon
¹/₄ teaspoon salt
¹/₃ cup unsalted butter, room temperature
³/₄ cup, plus 2 tablespoons sugar
1 large egg
³/₄ cup whole milk
1¹/₈ teaspoons vanilla extract

1. Preheat the oven at 300°F.

2. Line 12 muffin tin cups with paper cupcake liners.

3. Sift the flour, baking powder, cinnamon, and salt into a medium bowl.

4. In an electric mixer, or large bowl, beat the butter until light and fluffy, and then gradually add in the sugar and mix well.

5. Beat in the egg until well blended.

6. Measure the milk into a separate bowl and add the vanilla.

7. Reduce speed to low, and add the flour mixture and milk alternately in three steps to the butter mixture, beginning and ending with flour. Beat until smooth.

8. Pour the batter into the lined cupcake pan, distributing the batter equally.

9. Bake for 10 minutes, rotate, and bake for 12 more minutes or until a toothpick inserted in the center of a cupcake comes out clean.

10. Place the pan on a wire rack, and cool completely.

Sweet Vanilla Cupcakes
Makes 12 cupcakes

1½ cups cake flour
1 teaspoon baking powder
¼ teaspoon salt
⅓ cup unsalted butter, room temperature
⅔ cup, plus 3 tablespoons sugar
1 large egg
1 teaspoon vanilla extract
¼ vanilla bean, seeds only
⅔ cup whole milk

1. Preheat the oven to 300°F.

2. Line 12 muffin tin cups with paper cupcake liners.

3. Sift flour, baking powder, and salt together in a medium bowl.

4. In an electric mixer, or large bowl, beat the butter until light and fluffy and then gradually add in the sugar and mix well.

5. Beat in the egg until well blended, and then beat in the vanilla extract.

6. Slice the vanilla bean in half, lengthwise and scrape out the seeds using a paring knife. Discard the husk.

7. Measure the milk into a small container and add the vanilla seeds.

8. Add the flour mixture and milk alternately in three steps to the butter mixture, beginning and ending with flour. Blend gently until smooth.

9. Pour the batter into the lined cupcake pan, distributing the batter equally.

10. Bake for 10 minutes, rotate, and bake for 12 more minutes or until a toothpick inserted in the center of a cupcake comes out clean.

11. Place the pan on a wire rack, and cool completely.

Vegan Chocolate Cupcakes

Makes 12 cupcakes

¾ cup all-purpose flour
2 tablespoons cocoa powder
¼ teaspoon baking soda
½ cup sugar
½ cup water
4 tablespoons canola oil
1½ teaspoons white vinegar
1 teaspoon vanilla extract

1. Preheat the oven to 350°F.

2. Line 12 muffin tin cups with paper cupcake liners.

3. Sift the flour, cocoa powder, baking soda, and sugar into a medium bowl.

4. In an electric mixer, or large bowl, beat the water, oil, vinegar, and vanilla extract until well blended.

5. Reduce speed to low and add the flour mixture and beat until smooth.

6. Pour the batter into the lined cupcake pan, distributing the batter equally.

7. Bake for 10 minutes, rotate, and bake for 15 more minutes or until a toothpick inserted in the center of a cupcake comes out clean.

8. Place the pan on a wire rack, and cool completely.

Frosting: It's Tops!

Cappuccino Frosting
Caramel Buttercream Frosting
Chocolate Buttercream Frosting
Chocolate Ganache Frosting
Cinnamon Buttercream Frosting
Coconut Buttercream Frosting
Cookie Buttercream Frosting
Cream Cheese Frosting
Ginger Buttercream Frosting
Green Mint Buttercream Frosting
Lemon Buttercream Frosting
Maple Buttercream Frosting
Orange Spice Buttercream Frosting
Peppermint Buttercream Frosting
Vanilla Buttercream Frosting
Vegan Chocolate Frosting
Whipped Cream Frosting

Some say frosting is the best part of the cupcake. These are the same people who lick the frosting clean off the top and leave a sad, lonely lump of cake. If you are one of these people, this chapter is for you!

Cappuccino Frosting
Makes enough for 12 cupcakes

1 cup, plus 2 tablespoons cream cheese, room temperature
6 tablespoons unsalted butter, room temperature
4 cups confectioners sugar
2¼ teaspoons cinnamon
2¼ teaspoons vanilla extract
2¼ teaspoons liquid coffee flavor

1. In an electric mixer, or large bowl, beat the cream cheese and butter on medium speed until creamy.

2. In a separate bowl, sift the confectioners sugar and cinnamon together.

3. Add the confectioners sugar mixture, one cup at a time, to the butter mixture on low speed until it begins to incorporate.

4. Add the vanilla extract and coffee flavor.

5. Let the mixer run at low speed for a few minutes, then increase to medium speed very briefly to blend to desired consistency.

Caramel Buttercream Frosting

Makes enough for 12 cupcakes

1/4 *vanilla bean, seeds only*
1/2 *cup unsalted butter, room temperature*
1/2 *cup trans fat-free vegetable shortening*
2 *cups confectioners sugar*
2 *tablespoons caramel sauce*
3/4 *teaspoon vanilla extract*

1. Slice the vanilla bean in half lengthwise and scrape out the seeds using a paring knife. Discard the husk, and set the seeds aside.

2. In an electric mixer, or large bowl, beat the butter and vegetable shortening on medium speed until creamy.

3. Add the vanilla seeds and mix for a few seconds on medium speed.

4. In a separate bowl, sift the confectioners sugar.

5. Add the confectioners sugar to the butter mixture on low speed until it begins to incorporate.

6. Warm the caramel sauce (make sure it is warm, not hot).

7. Add the warmed caramel sauce and vanilla extract, and beat at medium to high speed until fully incorporated.

Chocolate Buttercream Frosting

Makes enough for 12 cupcakes

½ cup unsalted butter, room temperature
½ cup trans fat-free vegetable shortening
1¾ cups confectioners sugar
¼ cup cocoa powder
¼ teaspoon vanilla extract

1. In an electric mixer, or large bowl, beat the butter and vegetable shortening on medium speed until creamy.

2. In a separate bowl, sift the confectioners sugar and the cocoa powder together.

3. Add the confectioners sugar and the cocoa powder to the butter mixture on low speed until it begins to incorporate.

4. Add the vanilla extract, and beat at medium to high speed until fully incorporated.

Chocolate Ganache Frosting
Makes enough for 12 cupcakes

1 pound bittersweet or dark chocolate, broken into small
*   pieces*
8 ounces heavy cream

1. Put small bits of chocolate into a heat resistant bowl
    that is big enough to accommodate the cream, and
    set aside.

2. Heat the cream in a heavy-bottomed saucepan until
    it boils gently.

3. Pour the hot cream over the chocolate.

4. Cover with a plate or plastic wrap, and let stand 10
    minutes, stirring occasionally until smooth.

5. Frost the cupcakes immediately while the ganache
    is still warm.

Cinnamon Buttercream Frosting
Makes enough for 12 cupcakes

½ cup unsalted butter, room temperature
½ cup trans fat-free vegetable shortening
2 cups confectioners sugar
1 tablespoon cinnamon
1½ teaspoons vanilla extract

1. In an electric mixer, or large bowl, beat the butter and vegetable shortening on medium speed until creamy.

2. In a separate bowl, sift the confectioners sugar and cinnamon together.

3. Add the confectioners sugar mixture to the butter mixture on low speed until it begins to incorporate.

4. Add the vanilla extract, and beat at medium to high speed until fully incorporated.

Coconut Buttercream Frosting

Makes enough for 12 cupcakes

¼ vanilla bean, seeds only
½ cup unsalted butter, room temperature
½ cup trans fat-free vegetable shortening
2 cups confectioners sugar
¾ teaspoon vanilla extract
¾ teaspoon natural coconut flavor

1. Slice the vanilla bean in half lengthwise and scrape out the seeds using a paring knife. Discard the husk, and set the seeds aside.

2. In an electric mixer, or large bowl, beat the butter and vegetable shortening on medium speed until creamy.

3. Add the vanilla seeds and mix for a few seconds on medium speed.

4. In a separate bowl, sift the confectioners sugar.

5. Add the confectioners sugar to the butter mixture on low speed until it begins to incorporate.

6. Add the vanilla extract and coconut flavor, and beat at medium to high speed until fully incorporated.

Cookie Buttercream Frosting
Makes enough for 12 cupcakes

$\frac{1}{2}$ cup unsalted butter, room temperature
$\frac{1}{2}$ cup trans fat-free vegetable shortening
2 cups confectioners sugar
2 tablespoons crushed chocolate cookie bits (packaged chocolate cookies, such as Oreo cookies, filling removed)
$1\frac{1}{2}$ teaspoons vanilla extract

1. In an electric mixer, or large bowl, beat the butter and vegetable shortening on medium speed until creamy.

2. In a separate bowl, sift the confectioners sugar.

3. Add the confectioners sugar and crushed cookie bits to the butter mixture on low speed until it begins to incorporate.

4. Add the vanilla extract, and beat at medium to high speed until fully incorporated.

Cream Cheese Frosting
Makes enough for 12 cupcakes

1 cup, plus 2 tablespoons cream cheese, room temperature
6 tablespoons unsalted butter, room temperature
4 cups confectioners sugar
2¼ teaspoons vanilla extract

1. In an electric mixer, or large bowl, beat the cream cheese and butter on medium speed until creamy.

2. In a separate bowl, sift the confectioners sugar.

3. Add the confectioners sugar to the butter mixture on low speed until it begins to incorporate.

4. Add the vanilla extract, and beat at medium to high speed until fully incorporated.

Ginger Buttercream Frosting

Makes enough for 12 cupcakes

¼ vanilla bean, seeds only
½ cup unsalted butter, room temperature
½ cup trans fat-free vegetable shortening
2 cups confectioners sugar
1 tablespoon ground ginger
¾ teaspoon vanilla extract

1. Slice the vanilla bean in half lengthwise and scrape out the seeds using a paring knife. Discard the husk, and set the seeds aside.

2. In an electric mixer, or large bowl, beat the butter and vegetable shortening on medium speed until creamy.

3. Add the vanilla seeds and mix for a few seconds on medium speed.

4. In a separate bowl, sift the confectioners sugar.

5. Add the confectioners sugar to the butter mixture on low speed until it begins to incorporate.

6. Add the ground ginger and vanilla extract, and beat at medium to high speed until fully incorporated.

Green Mint Buttercream Frosting

Makes enough for 12 cupcakes

¼ vanilla bean, seeds only
½ cup unsalted butter, room temperature
½ cup trans fat-free vegetable shortening
2 cups confectioners sugar
¾ teaspoon vanilla extract
¾ teaspoon natural peppermint flavor
Green food coloring

1. Slice the vanilla bean in half lengthwise and scrape out the seeds using a paring knife. Discard the husk, and set the seeds aside.

2. In an electric mixer, or large bowl, beat the butter and vegetable shortening on medium speed until creamy.

3. Add the vanilla seeds and mix for a few seconds on medium speed.

4. In a separate bowl, sift the confectioners sugar.

5. Add the confectioners sugar to the butter mixture on low speed until it begins to incorporate.

6. Add the vanilla extract and peppermint flavor, and beat at medium to high speed until fully incorporated.

7. Hand-stir the green food coloring in, drop by drop, until you achieve your desired shade of light green.

Lemon Buttercream Frosting

Makes enough for 12 cupcakes

¼ vanilla bean, seeds only
½ cup unsalted butter, room temperature
½ cup trans fat-free vegetable shortening
2 cups confectioners sugar
¾ teaspoon vanilla extract
¾ teaspoon natural lemon flavor

1. Slice the vanilla bean in half lengthwise and scrape out the seeds using a paring knife. Discard the husk, and set the seeds aside.

2. In an electric mixer, or large bowl, beat the butter and vegetable shortening on medium speed until creamy.

3. Add the vanilla seeds and mix for a few seconds on medium speed.

4. In a separate bowl, sift the confectioners sugar.

5. Add the confectioners sugar to the butter mixture on low speed until it begins to incorporate.

6. Add the vanilla extract and lemon flavor, and beat at medium to high speed until fully incorporated.

Maple Buttercream Frosting

Makes enough for 12 cupcakes

¼ vanilla bean, seeds only
½ cup unsalted butter, room temperature
½ cup trans fat-free vegetable shortening
2 cups confectioners sugar
¾ teaspoon vanilla extract
¾ teaspoon natural maple flavor

1. Slice the vanilla bean in half lengthwise and scrape out the seeds using a paring knife. Discard the husk, and set the seeds aside.

2. In an electric mixer, or large bowl, beat the butter and vegetable shortening on medium speed until creamy.

3. Add the vanilla seeds and mix for a few seconds on medium speed.

4. In a separate bowl, sift the confectioners sugar.

5. Add the confectioners sugar to the butter mixture on low speed until it begins to incorporate.

6. Add the vanilla extract and maple flavor, and beat at medium to high speed until fully incorporated.

Orange Spice Buttercream Frosting
Makes enough for 12 cupcakes

½ cup unsalted butter, room temperature
½ cup trans fat-free vegetable shortening
2 cups confectioners sugar
1 teaspoon cinnamon
⅛ teaspoon nutmeg
⅛ teaspoon ground cloves
1½ teaspoons vanilla extract
1 tablespoon natural orange flavor

1. In an electric mixer, or large bowl, beat the butter and vegetable shortening on medium speed until creamy.

2. In a separate bowl, sift the confectioners sugar, cinnamon, nutmeg, and cloves together.

3. Add the confectioners sugar mixture to the butter mixture on low speed until it begins to incorporate.

4. Add the vanilla extract and orange flavor, and beat at medium to high speed until fully incorporated.

Peppermint Buttercream Frosting

Makes enough for 12 cupcakes

1/4 *vanilla bean, seeds only*
1/2 *cup unsalted butter, room temperature*
1/2 *cup trans fat-free vegetable shortening*
2 *cups confectioners sugar*
3/4 *teaspoon vanilla extract*
3/4 *teaspoon natural peppermint flavor*

1. Slice the vanilla bean in half lengthwise and scrape out the seeds using a paring knife. Discard the husk, and set the seeds aside.

2. In an electric mixer, or large bowl, beat the butter and vegetable shortening on medium speed until creamy.

3. Add the vanilla seeds and mix for a few seconds on medium speed.

4. In a separate bowl, sift the confectioners sugar.

5. Add the confectioners sugar to the butter mixture on low speed until it begins to incorporate.

6. Add the vanilla extract and peppermint flavor, and beat at medium to high speed until fully incorporated.

Vanilla Buttercream Frosting

Makes enough for 12 cupcakes

1/4 vanilla bean, seeds only
1/2 cup unsalted butter, room temperature
1/2 cup trans fat-free vegetable shortening
2 cups confectioners sugar
3/4 teaspoon vanilla extract

1. Slice the vanilla bean in half lengthwise and scrape out the seeds using a paring knife. Discard the husk, and set the seeds aside.

2. In an electric mixer, or large bowl, beat the butter and vegetable shortening on medium speed until creamy.

3. Add the vanilla seeds and mix for a few seconds on medium speed.

4. In a separate bowl, sift the confectioners sugar.

5. Add the confectioners sugar to the butter mixture on low speed until it begins to incorporate.

6. Add the vanilla extract, and beat at medium to high speed until fully incorporated.

Vegan Chocolate Frosting

Makes enough for 12 cupcakes

½ cup vegan butter or margarine, room temperature
½ cup trans fat-free vegetable shortening
1¾ cups confectioners sugar
¼ cup cocoa powder
¼ teaspoon vanilla extract

1. In an electric mixer, or large bowl, beat the butter and vegetable shortening on medium speed until creamy.

2. In a separate bowl, sift the confectioners sugar and cocoa powder together.

3. Add the confectioners sugar mixture to the butter mixture on low speed until it begins to incorporate.

4. Add the vanilla extract, and beat at medium to high speed until fully incorporated.

Whipped Cream Frosting

Makes enough for 12 cupcakes

⅓ cup confectioners sugar
3½ teaspoons whipped cream stabilizer*
2 cups heavy cream

1. In an electric mixer (fitted with a wire whip attachment), or a large bowl, add all ingredients and beat on low speed together. (Initially, there can be a lot of splatter, so you may want to begin whisking by hand.)

2. Mix on low speed until all ingredients are incorporated, and then turn up to high speed and mix until it is light and fluffy.

*Small packets of Whip it *(a common whipped cream stabilizer), made by Dr. Oetker, can be found in the baking aisle of grocery stores, or online.*

Cupcake Fillings

Banana Caramel Cream Filling
Berry Bash Jam
Blueberry Preserves
Cinnamon Apple Preserves
Cranberry Preserves
Key Lime Curd Filling
Pastry Cream Filling
Pineapple Preserves
Pomegranate Preserves
Raspberry Preserves
Rhubarb Preserves
Strawberry Preserves

This is where the real fun starts! These bells and whistles will wow guests, as you pull out new flavors, new looks, and a new-found respect in your baking abilities. From freshly-made jams to rich cream and curd fillings, you'll get your fill, for sure.

Tip: We recommend preparing any fillings the day before you plan to make your cupcakes. But if you need a quick way of cooling down any jams or fillings on the same day, pour the fillings into a cookie sheet and place it in the freezer for about 15 to 20 minutes.

Banana Caramel Cream Filling

Makes enough to fill 12 cupcakes

¾ cup light brown sugar, firmly packed
½ small ripe banana, peeled and cut into 1-inch pieces
1½ tablespoons unsalted butter, room temperature
1¾ cup plus 2 tablespoons chilled heavy cream, divided
¾ teaspoon plus ⅛ teaspoon whipped cream
*   stabilizer**
1 tablespoon confectioners sugar

1. Combine the brown sugar, banana, and butter in a food processor and blend until smooth.

2. Add ¾ cup of the heavy cream and blend. Transfer the mixture to a medium-sized, heavy-bottomed saucepan.

3. Whisk over medium heat until the sugar dissolves and the mixture boils. Attach a candy thermometer to the inside of the pan and cook, without stirring or swirling, until temperature registers 218°F (about 6 minutes).

4. Pour the caramel into a bowl. Cool to room temperature, whisking occasionally.

5. In a separate large bowl, whisk the remaining 1 cup, plus 2 tablespoons of heavy cream, whipped cream stabilizer, and confectioners sugar until cream mounds softly.

6. Gradually fold in the cool caramel mixture with a

spatula and let it cool slightly at room temperature. Then cover tightly with plastic wrap and chill until the cream is firm enough to spread (about 3 hours).

Small packets of Whip it *(a common whipped cream stabilizer), made by Dr. Oetker, can be found in the baking aisle of grocery stores, or online.*

Berry Bash Jam

Makes enough to fill 12 cupcakes

⅓ cup blackberries
⅓ cup raspberries
⅓ cup strawberries, de-stemmed
1¾ cups sugar
⅛ teaspoon unsalted butter
3 tablespoons liquid fruit pectin*

* Found in canning aisle of grocery store, or online. Do not use powdered pectin.

1. Chop the berries in a food processor until chopped into a chunky paste (you can use a potato masher if you do not have a food processor).

2. Put the fruit into a 6- or 8-quart saucepan and place on high heat.

3. Stir the sugar in with the fruit, and then add the butter.

4. Bring the mixture to a full rolling boil (a boil that doesn't stop bubbling when stirred) and keep on high heat, stirring constantly.

5. Stir in the pectin quickly and return to a full rolling boil for exactly 1 minute, stirring constantly.

6. Remove from the heat and pour into a heavy duty container (either plastic or glass), cover, and refrigerate.

Blueberry Preserves
Makes enough to fill 12 cupcakes

1 cup blueberries
1¾ cups sugar
⅛ teaspoon unsalted butter
3 tablespoons liquid fruit pectin*

* Found in canning aisle of grocery store, or online. Do not use powdered pectin.

1. Chop the blueberries in a food processor until chopped into a chunky paste (you can use a potato masher if you do not have a food processor).

2. Put the fruit into a 6- or 8-quart saucepan and place on high heat.

3. Stir the sugar in with the fruit, and then add the butter.

4. Bring the mixture to a full rolling boil (a boil that doesn't stop bubbling when stirred) and keep on high heat, stirring constantly.

5. Stir in the pectin quickly and return to a full rolling boil for exactly 1 minute, stirring constantly.

6. Remove from the heat and pour into a heavy duty container (either plastic or glass), cover, and refrigerate.

Cinnamon Apple Preserves

Makes enough to fill 12 cupcakes

1 cup apples, cored, peeled, and chopped
1¾ cups sugar
⅛ teaspoon unsalted butter
1½ tablespoons liquid fruit pectin*
2¼ teaspoons cinnamon

* Found in canning aisle of grocery store, or online. Do not use powdered pectin.

1. Chop the apples in a food processor until chopped into a chunky paste (you can use a potato masher if you do not have a food processor).

2. Put the fruit into a 6- or 8-quart saucepan and place on high heat.

3. Stir the sugar in with the fruit, and then add the butter.

4. Bring the mixture to a full rolling boil (a boil that doesn't stop bubbling when stirred) and keep on high heat, stirring constantly.

5. Stir in the pectin quickly and return to a full rolling boil for exactly 1 minute, stirring constantly.

6. Add the cinnamon and stir.

7. Remove from the heat and pour into a heavy duty container (either plastic or glass), cover, and refrigerate.

Cranberry Preserves
Makes enough to fill 12 cupcakes

1 cup cranberries
1¾ cups sugar
⅛ teaspoon unsalted butter
1½ tablespoons liquid fruit pectin*

* Found in canning aisle of grocery store, or online. Do not use powdered pectin.

1. Chop the berries in a food processor until chopped into a chunky paste (you can use a potato masher if you do not have a food processor).

2. Put the fruit into a 6- or 8-quart saucepan and place on high heat.

3. Stir the sugar in with the fruit, and then add the butter.

4. Bring the mixture to a full rolling boil (a boil that doesn't stop bubbling when stirred) and keep on high heat, stirring constantly.

5. Stir in the pectin quickly and return to a full rolling boil for exactly 1 minute, stirring constantly.

6. Remove from the heat and pour into a heavy duty container (either plastic or glass), cover, and refrigerate.

Key Lime Curd Filling

Makes enough to fill 12 cupcakes

¼ *cup lime juice*
¼ *cup unsalted butter*
2 *large eggs*
½ *cup sugar*

1. Mix all ingredients in a saucepan over medium to low heat.

2. Stir constantly until the mixture boils.

3. Chill uncovered, stirring every ten minutes until cooled.

4. When completely cooled (usually after about 20 minutes), cover and store in the refrigerator.

Pastry Cream Filling
Makes enough to fill 12 cupcakes

1 cup half and half
1/4 cup sugar, divided
2 large egg yolks
4 1/2 to 6 teaspoons cornstarch
2 tablespoons unsalted butter, cold and cut into 2 pieces
3/4 teaspoons vanilla extract

1. Heat the half and half and 3 tablespoons of the sugar in a heavy-bottomed saucepan over medium heat until simmering. Stir occasionally until the sugar is dissolved.

2. Meanwhile, whisk the egg yolks in a medium bowl until thoroughly combined.

3. Whisk in the remaining 1 tablespoon of sugar until pale and the sugar has begun to dissolve. The mixture should be creamy.

4. Whisk in 4½ teaspoons of cornstarch until combined and the mixture is pale yellow and thick. You may need to add another teaspoon of cornstarch to make it a little stiffer.

5. When the half and half mixture reaches a full simmer, gradually whisk this into the egg yolks mixture to temper.

6. Return the mixture to the saucepan, scraping the bowl with a rubber spatula. Return to simmer over

medium heat, whisking constantly until a few bubbles burst on the surface and the mixture is thickened and glossy (approx. 30 seconds).

7. Move the saucepan off the heat, and whisk in the butter and vanilla.

8. Strain the pastry cream through a fine mesh sieve set over a medium bowl.

9. Press plastic wrap directly onto the surface of the cream and refrigerate for at least 3 hours (up to 2 days).

Pineapple Preserves
Makes enough to fill 12 cupcakes

1 cup crushed pineapple (canned), strained of excess juice
1¾ cups sugar
⅛ teaspoon unsalted butter
3 tablespoons liquid fruit pectin*

* Found in canning aisle of grocery store, or online. Do not use powdered pectin.

1. Put the fruit into a 6- or 8-quart saucepan and place on high heat.

2. Stir the sugar in with the fruit, and then add the butter.

3. Bring the mixture to a full rolling boil (a boil that doesn't stop bubbling when stirred) and keep on high heat, stirring constantly.

4. Stir in the pectin quickly and return to a full rolling boil for exactly 1 minute, stirring constantly.

5. Remove from the heat and pour into a heavy duty container (either plastic or glass), cover, and refrigerate.

Pomegranate Preserves
Makes enough to fill 12 cupcakes

1¼ cup pomegranate seeds
1¾ cups sugar
⅛ teaspoon unsalted butter
1½ tablespoons liquid fruit pectin*

* Found in canning aisle of grocery store, or online. Do not use powdered pectin.

1. Chop the pomegranate seeds in a food processor until they are chopped into a chunky paste (you can use a potato masher if you do not have a food processor).

2. Put the fruit into a 6- or 8-quart saucepan and place on high heat.

3. Stir the sugar in with the fruit, and then add the butter.

4. Bring the mixture to a full rolling boil (a boil that doesn't stop bubbling when stirred) and keep on high heat, stirring constantly.

5. Stir in the pectin quickly and return to a full rolling boil for exactly 1 minute, stirring constantly.

6. Remove from the heat and pour into a heavy duty container (either plastic or glass), cover, and refrigerate.

Raspberry Preserves
Makes enough to fill 12 cupcakes

1 cup raspberries
1¾ cups sugar
⅛ teaspoon unsalted butter
3 tablespoons liquid fruit pectin*

* Found in canning aisle of grocery store, or online. Do not use powdered pectin.

1. Chop the raspberries in a food processor until they are chopped into a chunky paste (you can use a potato masher if you do not have a food processor).

2. Put the fruit into a 6- or 8-quart saucepan and place on high heat.

3. Stir the sugar in with the fruit, and then add the butter.

4. Bring the mixture to a full rolling boil (a boil that doesn't stop bubbling when stirred) and keep on high heat, stirring constantly.

5. Stir in the pectin quickly and return to a full rolling boil for exactly one minute, stirring constantly.

6. Remove from the heat and pour into a heavy duty container (either plastic or glass), cover, and refrigerate.

Rhubarb Preserves
Makes enough to fill 12 cupcakes

1 cup rhubarb, chopped
1¾ cups sugar
⅛ teaspoon unsalted butter
3 tablespoons liquid fruit pectin*

*Found in canning aisle of grocery store, or online. Do not use powdered pectin.

1. Cut off the leafy parts of the rhubarb stalks, as well as the opposite tips. Then peel the rhubarb stalks and chop into small chunks.

2. Chop the rhubarb in a food processor until it is chopped into a chunky paste (you can use a potato masher if you do not have a food processor).

3. Put the fruit into a 6- or 8-quart saucepan and place on high heat.

4. Stir the sugar in with the fruit, and then add the butter.

5. Bring the mixture to a full rolling boil (a boil that doesn't stop bubbling when stirred) and keep on high heat, stirring constantly.

6. Stir in the pectin quickly and return to a full rolling boil for exactly one minute, stirring constantly.

7. Remove from the heat and pour into a heavy duty container (either plastic or glass), cover, and refrigerate.

Strawberry Preserves
Makes enough to fill 12 cupcakes

1 cup strawberries, de-stemmed
1³/₄ cups sugar
¹/₈ teaspoon unsalted butter
1¹/₂ tablespoons liquid fruit pectin*

Found in canning aisle of grocery store, or online. Do not use powdered pectin.

1. Chop the berries in a food processor until chopped into a chunky paste (you can use a potato masher if you do not have a food processor).

2. Put the fruit into a 6- or 8-quart saucepan and place on high heat.

3. Stir the sugar in with the fruit, and then add the butter.

4. Bring the mixture to a full rolling boil (a boil that doesn't stop bubbling when stirred) and keep on high heat, stirring constantly.

5. Stir in the pectin quickly and return to a full rolling boil for exactly 1 minute, stirring constantly.

6. Remove from the heat and pour into a heavy duty container (either plastic or glass), cover, and refrigerate.